Challenges of Conflicting School Reforms

Effects of New American Schools in a High-Poverty District

Mark Berends, JoAn Chun, Gina Schuyler
Sue Stockly, and R. J. Briggs

Supported by

New American Schools

RAND
EDUCATION

The research described in this report was supported by New American Schools.

ISBN: 0-8330-3116-3

RAND is a nonprofit institution that helps improve policy and decisionmaking through research and analysis. RAND® is a registered trademark. RAND's publications do not necessarily reflect the opinions or policies of its research sponsors.

Cover design by Stephen Bloodsworth

Published 2002 by RAND
1700 Main Street, P.O. Box 2138, Santa Monica, CA 90407-2138
1200 South Hayes Street, Arlington, VA 22202-5050
201 North Craig Street, Suite 102, Pittsburgh, PA 15213-1516
RAND URL: http://www.rand.org/
To order RAND documents or to obtain additional information, contact Distribution Services: Telephone: (310) 451-7002;
Fax: (310) 451-6915; Email: order@rand.org

As a private nonprofit corporation, New American Schools (NAS) began in 1991 to fund the development of designs aimed at transforming entire schools at the elementary and secondary levels. Having completed competition and development phases, NAS currently is scaling-up its designs across the nation. During the phase when NAS was committed to implementing its designs across schools within partnering jurisdictions, RAND's research assessed the impact of NAS designs on classroom practice and student achievement in a sample of schools in a high-poverty district during the 1997–1998 and 1998–1999 school years.

The current study is aimed at those who want to better understand the expanding area of whole-school, or comprehensive, school reform and its effects on teaching and learning within high-stakes accountability environments.

RAND's assessment of NAS schools has spanned several years. To date, RAND studies about New American Schools include:

Implementation in a Longitudinal Sample of New American Schools: Four Years into Scale-Up, by Sheila Nataraj Kirby, Mark Berends, and Scott Naftel, 2001 (MR-1413-EDU).

The Relationship Between Implementation and Achievement: Case Studies of New American Schools, by JoAn Chun, Brian Gill, and Jodi Heilbrunn, forthcoming (DRU-2562-EDU).

"Reforming Whole Schools: Challenges and Complexities," by Mark Berends, Susan Bodily, and Sheila Nataraj Kirby. Forthcoming in *Bringing Equity Back,* edited by J. Petrovich and A. W. Wells.

"Leadership in Districts and Schools Required to Successfully Use Comprehensive School Designs," by Mark Berends, Susan Bodilly, and Sheila Kirby. Forthcoming in *Leadership in School Reform: Lessons from Comprehensive School Reform Designs,* edited by Joseph Murphy and Amanda Datnow.

Implementation and Performance in New American Schools: Three Years into Scale-Up, by Mark Berends, Sheila N. Kirby, Scott Naftel, and Christopher McKelvey, 2001 (MR-1145-EDU).

New American Schools' Concept of Break the Mold Designs: How Designs Evolved Over Time and Why, by Susan Bodilly, 2001 (MR-1288-NAS).

"Teacher-Reported Effects of New American Schools' Designs: Exploring Relationships to Teacher Background and School Context," by Mark Berends in *Educational Evaluation and Policy Analysis,* 2000, 22(1), 65–82.

"Necessary District Support for Comprehensive School Reform," by Susan J. Bodilly and Mark Berends. Pp. 111–119 in *Hard Work for Good Schools: Facts Not Fads in Title I Reform,* edited by Gary Orfield and Elizabeth H. DeBray. Boston, MA: Civil Rights Project, Harvard University, 1999.

Assessing the Progress of New American Schools: A Status Report, by Mark Berends, 1999 (MR-1085-ED).

Lessons from New American Schools' Scale-Up Phase: Prospects for Bringing Designs to Multiple Schools, by Susan J. Bodilly, 1998 (MR-1777-NAS).

New American Schools After Six Years, by Thomas K. Glennan, Jr., 1998 (MR-945-NASDC).

Funding Comprehensive School Reform, by Brent R. Keltner, 1998 (IP-175-EDU).

Reforming America's Schools: Observations on Implementing "Whole School Designs," by Susan J. Bodilly and Thomas K. Glennan, 1998 (RB-8016-EDU).

Lessons from New American Schools Development Corporation's Demonstration Phase, by Susan J. Bodilly, 1996 (MR-729-NASDC).

Reforming and Conforming: NASDC Principals Discuss School Accountability Systems, by Karen Mitchell, 1996 (MR-716-NASDC).

"Lessons Learned from RAND's Formative Assessment of NASDC's Phase 2 Demonstration Effort" by Susan J. Bodilly. Pp. 289–324 in *Bold Plans for School Restructuring: The New American Schools Designs,* edited by Sam Stringfield, Steven Ross, and Lana Smith. Mahwah, NJ: Lawrence Erlbaum Associates, 1996.

Designing New American Schools: Baseline Observations on Nine Design Teams, by Susan J. Bodilly, Susanna Purnell, Kimberly Ramsey, and Christina Smith, 1995 (MR-598-NASDC).

Funding for this research was provided under a contract with NAS and supported by the Ford Foundation and another donor. This report was written under the aegis of RAND Education.

CONTENTS

FIGURES

TABLES

A decade ago, New American Schools (NAS) launched an ambitious effort for whole-school reform to address the perceived lagging achievement of American students and the lackluster school reform attempts that produced so little meaningful change. As a private non-profit organization, NAS set out to help schools and districts significantly raise the achievement of large numbers of students by offering whole-school designs and design-based assistance during the implementation process. NAS is currently in the scale-up phase of its effort and its designs are being widely diffused to schools across the nation.

The purpose of this study is to examine the conditions of NAS classrooms compared with non-NAS classrooms and to study the relationships between classroom conditions and student achievement in a high-poverty district in San Antonio, Texas. The focus is on the conditions in the district, schools, and classrooms that promote or inhibit design implementation and changes in teaching and learning.

Specifically, this study addresses the following questions:

- Do the NAS designs extend beyond changes in school organization and governance and permeate classrooms? Do NAS teachers and students interact with each other and subject materials in ways that reflect the innovative curricular and instructional approaches of the design teams?

- What factors at the district, school, and classroom level are related to implementation of designs, changes in classroom instruction, and student achievement?

In this report, we are not attempting a "summative" evaluation, thereby claiming that the NAS designs have been thoroughly developed and implemented so that program effects can be clearly detected. Such an evaluation seems premature, given the variation in implementation among designs between different sites, the support and leadership provided by districts, and the different stages of design implementation and development (see Berends and Kirby et al., 2001; Bodilly, 2001; Kirby, Berends, and Naftel, 2001). Rather, our intent is more "formative" in order to provide empirical results and insights to educators and policymakers who are interested in whole-school or comprehensive school reform, particularly in high-poverty schools within high-stakes accountability environments.

THE ANALYSIS SAMPLE

The schools included in this study were those involved in the early stages of the San Antonio district's partnership with NAS. The NAS designs being implemented in this district at the time of this study included Co-NECT, Expeditionary Learning/Outward Bound (ELOB), Modern Red Schoolhouse (MRSH), and Success for All/Roots & Wings (SFA/RW).[1]

We gathered a variety of data, including: principal and teacher surveys conducted at the end of the 1997–1998 and 1998–1999 school years; interviews with district staff, design team leaders, local facilitators, principals, and teachers; classroom observations; illustrative examples of student work; data provided by the district on test scores and student and teacher demographic characteristics; and achievement data from a supplementary test administered to students (Stanford-9 reading). In addition, this study relies on other RAND research on NAS that included site visits to schools and school districts to gather information about district and school administrators' and

---

[1]While SFA has been around for the past couple of decades, NAS provided funding to the Success for All Foundation to develop and implement Roots & Wings, which not only includes the reading program of SFA, but also builds in other curricular programs such as MathWings and WorldLab. San Antonio schools were only implementing the SFA component of SFA/RW during the time of this study. Because the Success for All Foundation considers all SFA schools as potential RW schools and because NAS provided funding for RW, we refer to this design as SFA/RW.

teachers' reports of the progress of the NAS initiative (Berends and Kirby et al., 2001; Bodilly, 1998, 2001).

RAND collected these data on a sample of fourth grade teachers and their students during two school years. For analyzing changes in teacher practice between the 1997–1998 and 1998–1999 school years, we relied on a longitudinal sample of 40 teachers. In 1997–1998, we were also able to observe and gather classroom artifacts from 12 teachers in NAS and non-NAS schools, and in the following year, we were able to gather such data from 19 teachers. The analysis sample relating classroom conditions to student achievement consisted of over 60 teachers and roughly 850 students, but we also compared our results with all elementary schools and fourth grade teachers and students within the district.

IMPORTANT LIMITATIONS

There are several important limitations of this research that need to be kept in mind. First, for most design teams, the schools analyzed in this study were the first buildings to which they provided implementation assistance on a fee-for-service basis. Many changes have been made to both the designs and the assistance provided as the teams and the schools have gained experience (see Bodilly, 2001). Thus, when interpreting the findings in this report, it is important to note the unique features of the population of schools we studied.

Second, the fact that designs are evolving over time as design teams gain experience and adapt to local contexts may make future implementations more successful. However, this is still an open question, and some of our research calls this into question (Kirby, Berends, and Naftel, 2001). Certainly, additional empirical work would be helpful to address this issue.

Third, the district context in which these schools were implementing has changed dramatically since the time the data for this report were collected. Similar to many urban contexts, the superintendent and key staff have moved on to other positions, and some new district policies have been put in place. Whether these are more or less conducive to NAS design implementation is beyond the scope of the current analysis.

NAS WITHIN A REFORM-MINDED URBAN SCHOOL DISTRICT

As is evident in our description of these schools and classrooms within an urban school district, NAS partnered with schools and jurisdictions that are predominantly low-performing, urban, high poverty, and high minority (Berends and Kirby et al., 2001; Berends, 1999).

While NAS was busy starting up in July of 1991, the San Antonio school district struggled to raise its students' achievement levels and meet the challenges it faced. At the time, productive communication proved problematic, as did the effective utilization of district staff. Much energy was expended on the management of day-to-day organizational affairs. According to several central office administrators, instructional practice was too often last addressed.

When the new superintendent came on board in 1994, there were significant changes in the district that occurred. The superintendent proceeded to draw up five district goals: (1) increase student achievement; (2) foster collaboration and communication; (3) strengthen parent and community involvement; (4) build an infrastructure for professional development; and (5) provide appropriate school facilities to all students.

While restructuring instructional leadership, rethinking the delivery and content of professional development, introducing instructional strategies to teachers, pushing state standards, and refocusing the district's attention on instruction and student achievement, San Antonio district administrators simultaneously reviewed national reform efforts and programs. Central office administrators seriously examined and eventually decided to implement the reform ideas of NAS—particularly NAS's approach to comprehensive school reform. Convinced that the designs could play an important role in the district's efforts to bring about increased student achievement, the district considered the NAS designs an important piece of the reform package. Viewing NAS designs as the framework and glue to hold the multiple district initiatives together, the central office expected to monitor the progress of design implementation and support the schools in their efforts.

NAS IMPLEMENTATION IN SCHOOLS FACING HIGH-STAKES ACCOUNTABILITY

The district introduced the NAS initiative to schools with hopes that the marketed "break the mold" designs would provoke teachers and administrators to engage enthusiastically in comprehensive school reform. The thought was that an external model provider would be more successful at pushing and sustaining change than the central office could ever be alone. The district had every intention of fully supporting its NAS schools in all ways—including professional development, site-based facilitators (called Instructional Guides), and other resources for the schools to implement the designs.

Given this support, when NAS designs were first introduced in 1996, one might have expected that in time, design schools would look, feel, and in some ways function differently from one another as well as from schools that had elected not to take on a whole-school design.

Yet, this expectation was not met because of the many challenges faced by the district, schools, design teams, and teachers. A closer examination of both whole-school and individual classroom activities revealed a more complicated story. In our research we focused on the challenging educational environments that these schools faced, the high-stakes accountability system in which they operated, the process for adopting NAS designs, support for implementation including training and professional development, principal leadership, and teacher collaboration and support of the NAS designs.

The press to improve test scores on the state tests (Texas Assessment of Academic Skills [TAAS]) was clearly evident during the time of our study. For instance, in addition to the NAS designs, the district established an Office of Curriculum and Instruction responsible for developing a sequential, standards-aligned curriculum across grade levels in all schools throughout the district. The subjects covered on the TAAS, namely mathematics and reading, were given primary attention. Thus, schools were not only exposed to many ideas at the same time, but they were also required to implement them all at once, naturally resulting in some confusion and resistance on the part of school staff.

To address the demands of the TAAS, the district implemented specific mathematics, reading, and language arts programs in addition to the NAS designs. In the spring of 1996, all schools were implementing *Everyday Mathematics*—developed by the University of Chicago School Mathematics Project. The district expectations were that all schools throughout the district would follow a similar pace, and the district developed pacing guides to ensure that this would happen. In addition, San Antonio elementary schools began implementing a reading initiative that involved a 90-minute block of time. By the 1998–1999 school year, not only were elementary schools, district wide, expected to schedule two 90-minute blocks of uninterrupted instructional time for reading and math, respectively, teachers were required to manage time within these blocks in prescribed ways. Though not to the same degree, the district structured language arts activities (spelling, grammar, and writing) as well, totaling approximately 70 minutes of instruction time per day. Thus, roughly four hours of instructional activities were mapped out for all the district's elementary school teachers to follow (SFA/RW teachers were exempt from implementing the district's reading initiative).

In addition, lack of time during the school day—a chronic issue— became even more problematic in light of teachers' needs to balance TAAS preparation with other instruction. Many teachers stated in their interviews with us that they coped with the multiple demands on their time by putting aside other activities to focus almost exclusively on TAAS as the test dates grew closer.

Within this context, the district provided a substantial amount of professional development to teachers. Much of the in-service training revolved around the district's reading and mathematics initiatives. Because NAS teachers were obligated to attend as many of these various in-services as their colleagues in non-NAS schools, the amount of training activities served only to heighten frustrations. All of the designs except SFA/RW required teachers to develop units and write curriculum. While encouraging schools to implement NAS designs, the district simultaneously constrained their ability to do so by telling teachers what to teach and how.

The district and design teams did not tend to coordinate their efforts with respect to professional development, so teachers were left on their own to merge the information they received from each. This was not easily done without modifying the essence of each design. Not only did this effort burden teachers' workload, it also led to confusion as to what to prioritize.

Amid the professional development from the district, design teams were also assisting schools that adopted designs. Each NAS design team aims to provide schools and teachers with resources to assist in implementation, especially in terms of communication between design team members and school staff, and design-related professional development. For instance, by 1999 a relatively high proportion of teachers in the NAS schools (88 percent) agreed that their respective design teams had clearly communicated "its program to school staff so that it could be well-implemented."

Part of this communication involves teacher training by design teams. However, according to teachers across design schools, there was little regular, consistent assistance provided. Over time, there was even less contact between teachers and their respective design representatives. In large part, this had to do with the fact that these representatives serviced numerous schools, making it difficult for them to be attentive to any one. It also appears that from the start, strong relationships rarely were established, making it unlikely that teachers would rely on their respective design representatives for external technical support and assistance. In some schools, design representatives turned over, disrupting what rapport had been established.

CLASSROOM CONDITIONS IN NAS AND NON-NAS SCHOOLS

Our analyses revealed few differences in teacher perceptions of instructional environments between NAS and non-NAS schools. Some changes were evident. For example, about half of the teachers in NAS schools reported that they used reform-like practices (e.g., discussion in small groups to find a joint solution to a problem, project-based learning, use of manipulatives) at least once or twice a week compared with roughly one-third of non-NAS teachers. In other areas, fewer differences were found. For instance, both NAS and non-NAS teachers reported similar use of instructional materials, though more teachers in NAS than non-NAS schools perceived inadequate materials to be a problem. The more substantial differences we found were not between NAS and non-NAS schools, but between 1998 and 1999, which is likely a reflection of the dramatic level of change within the district itself. That is, while the implementation of NAS designs was not high relative to other schools and jurisdictions (see Berends and Kirby et al., 2001; Kirby et al., 2001), implementation of NAS designs was higher in 1998 than it was in 1999.

STUDENT ACHIEVEMENT IN NAS AND NON-NAS CLASSROOMS

Because instructional conditions varied more between NAS and non-NAS schools during the 1997–1998 school year, we analyzed data for that school year to examine whether such variation in instructional conditions was related to student achievement, controlling for other student, teacher, classroom, and school characteristics. We first examined relationships in all the fourth grade classrooms in the district and then in the sample of classrooms for which RAND gathered additional survey data on classroom instruction and a supplemental reading test (Stanford-9).

As expected because of the early stages of implementation, NAS designs had no significant effects on student achievement. More important, we did not find that instructional conditions promoted by reforms such as NAS—including teacher-reported collaboration, quality of professional development, and reform-like instructional practices—were related to student achievement net of other student and classroom conditions.

However, we did find significant effects of principal leadership on the TAAS reading and mathematics scores. Principal leadership in our analysis was measured by teacher reports about principals who clearly communicated what was expected of teachers, were supportive and encouraging of staff, obtained resources for the school, enforced rules for student conduct, talked with teachers regarding instructional practices, had confidence in the expertise of the teachers, and took a personal interest in the professional development of teachers. Our previous analyses have shown the importance of principal leadership in implementing the designs (Berends and Kirby et al., 2001; Kirby et al., 2001). Here we found a positive link between principal leadership and student performance in both NAS and non-NAS schools, indicating that leadership is important to achievement in general, and to implementation in particular.

POLICY IMPLICATIONS

Currently, many schools across the country are attempting NAS-like reforms using funding provided by such federal programs as Title I and the Comprehensive School Reform Demonstration (CSRD) program. Our study in conjunction with the other RAND studies on NAS has clear implications. Schools attempting comprehensive school reforms face many obstacles during implementation, and because of this, whole-school designs face continuing challenges in significantly raising the achievement of all students. This is particularly important to remember when setting expectations for school improvement under new federal, state, and local programs—particularly when implementing strategies and interventions in high-poverty, low-performing settings.

Because the target of the federal Title I and CSRD funds is primarily high-poverty schools, the schools most likely to be affected by the CSRD program are the same schools that are most likely to face a multitude of other difficulties. High-poverty schools often present very fragmented and conflicting environments with difficult and changing political currents and entrenched unions. Teachers in high-poverty schools often face new accountability systems as well as a fluctuating reform agenda, and generally lack sufficient time for implementing reform efforts, often becoming demoralized, losing their enthusiasm for the difficult task of improving student performance under difficult conditions (for a description of CSRD schools see Kirby et al., in review).

Federal and state policymakers need to think critically about their current stance of simultaneously promoting: high-stakes testing; the implementation of comprehensive school reforms that promote innovative curriculum and instructional strategies; and the implementation of multiple other concurrent reforms. The implementation of high-stakes testing regimes—the apparent outcome of many standards-based reforms—might preclude the adoption of rich and varied curricula that challenge students and motivate them toward more in-depth learning experiences. It certainly prevents such adoption when other more basic skills instructional reforms are mandated on top of the design-based curriculum. The current study shows that high-stakes tests may be a two-edged sword in this environment. On the one hand, high-stakes tests may motivate schools to increase performance and often to seek out new curricula and instructional strategies associated with comprehensive school reforms. On the other hand, those very same tests may provide disincentives to adopt richer, more in-depth curricula.

Our findings are consistent with Porter and Clune's scheme for better educational policy (Porter, 1994; Clune, 1998). They posit that educational policies such as comprehensive school reform are likely to influence teachers and students to the extent to which they are specific, powerful, authoritative, consistent, and stable. *Specificity*, or depth, is the extent to which the comprehensive school reform provides detailed guidance or materials to help schools and teachers understand what they are supposed to do (e.g., materials that describe the stages of implementing the design and ongoing, clear assistance strategies to further promote implementation). *Power* refers to the rewards or sanctions attached to the whole-school reform, such as teachers receiving bonuses or greater autonomy if they comply with implementing the design. *Authority* refers to the degree to which the reform policy is seen as *legitimate* and as having the *support* of those who are responsible for implementation. If respected groups or policymakers have strong positive views toward whole-school reform and if teachers support its implementation, the design is likely to have greater influence in changing teaching and learning. *Consistency* or *alignment* refers to the extent to which the set of whole-school interventions and strategies are aligned with a common mission and vision, within both the school and the district. *Stability* refers to the reform being sustained over time in a coherent, consistent manner. Policymakers and educators might use these dimensions as a means for thinking critically about the comprehensive school reform being considered and whether the conditions exist for it to succeed.

Thinking carefully about the factors necessary to promote high-quality implementation and coherence with other educational policies and reforms and ensuring that these factors are present and

aligned in schools is the only way in which comprehensive school reform can succeed in improving the learning opportunities of all students, particularly those in high-poverty settings.

ACKNOWLEDGMENTS

A research project such as this is never accomplished without the collaboration and cooperation of many people and organizations. We would like to thank the Ford Foundation and another donor for providing the research funding to New American Schools to support RAND's ongoing assessment. We are grateful to our reviewers, Amanda Datnow, University of Toronto, and Laura Hamilton of RAND. Their incisive reviews greatly benefited this study, in both substance and clarity.

We are also grateful to New American Schools, which deserves a special acknowledgment for supporting independent research on its efforts. We are also grateful to the students, teachers, principals, design teams, and district administrators and staff who allowed us in their schools and gave their time to respond to our questions, provided critical data, and clarified issues along the way. All played a crucial role in providing information to better understand what kinds of schools the NAS designs are working with, and we appreciate their efforts and dedication to improving the capacity of schools, the professional development of teachers, and the well-being of students.

We thank the members of the Research Advisory Panel (funded by the Annenberg Foundation) who provide critical guidance to RAND's research on NAS. Members include Barbara Cervone, Paul Hill, Janice Petrovich, Andrew Porter, Karen Sheingold, and Carol Weiss. We continue to learn from their experience, expertise, and encouragement. In addition, we are grateful to Tom Corcoran, Adam Gamoran, and Fred Newmann, who shared their expertise during the development of our principal and teacher surveys.

Several colleagues within RAND also contributed to the research underlying this report. Susan Bodilly, Co-Principal Investigator on RAND's program of NAS studies with Mark Berends, has been intimately involved in this research throughout. Sheila Nataraj Kirby, Senior Economist at RAND, and Thomas Glennan, senior advisor to this project, also provided helpful insights along the way.

Despite the cooperation, support, and guidance of these individuals and agencies, any errors in this report remain our own. The first four authors are listed alphabetically. Mark Berends was the principal investigator overseeing the study design, analysis, and integration of the reporting; JoAn Chun led the fieldwork, analyzed these qualitative data, and reported on the findings; Gina Schuyler was the project manager and helped coordinate the fieldwork, surveys, and student testing; Sue Stockly analyzed and reported on the survey information and student achievement analyses; and R. J. Briggs assisted in the data analysis on instruction and student achievement.

CSRD	Comprehensive School Reform Demonstration
EDM	Everyday Math of the University of Chicago
ELOB	Expeditionary Learning/Outward Bound
IG	Instructional Guide
ILT	Instructional Leadership Team
MRSH	Modern Red Schoolhouse
NAS	New American Schools
NASDC	New American Schools Development Corporation
RW	Roots & Wings
SAISD	San Antonio Independent School District
SALT	San Antonio Leadership Team
SFA	Success for All
SFA/RW	Success for All/Roots & Wings
Stanford-9	Stanford Open-Ended Reading Test, Version 9
TAAS	Texas Assessment of Academic Skills
TEA	Texas Education Agency
TEKS	Texas Education Knowledge Standards
TSSAS	Texas Successful Schools Award System

Chapter One

NEW AMERICAN SCHOOLS' AMBITIONS FOR CHANGING HIGH-POVERTY CLASSROOMS

New American Schools (NAS), a private non-profit organization, launched its efforts for whole-school reform in 1991 to address the common perception that our schools were failing students, particularly those in high-poverty settings, and that the piecemeal reform efforts had done little to improve the nation's educational system.

Based on the premise that high-quality schools can be established with external providers (design teams) supplying assistance to schools as they implement whole-school models of reform, NAS set out to help schools and districts significantly raise the achievement of large numbers of students.

SCALING UP NAS DESIGN TEAMS

As defined by NAS, a *design team* is an organization that provides high-quality, focused, ongoing professional development for teachers and administrators organized around a meaningful and compelling vision of what students should know and be able to do. The vision, or *design*, offers schools a focus for their improvement efforts, along with guidance in identifying what students need to know and be able to do and how to get there (New American Schools, 1997, p. 6). Glennan (1998, p. 11) describes a design further saying that it "articulates the school's vision, mission, and goals; guides the instructional program of the school; shapes the selection and socialization of the staff; and establishes common expectations for per-

1

formance, behavior, and accountability among students, teachers, and parents."

The intent of NAS's development of designs was to "design an educational environment to bring every child in this community up to world class standards in English, mathematics, science, history, and geography, prepared for responsible citizenship, further learning, and productive employment. No question about schooling should be off-limits; no answer assumed." Its interest was "in the comprehensive reformation of entire schools or sets of schools. [NAS] believes that all aspects of the school need to be integrated into a coherent, high-performance learning environment, a new American school" (New American Schools Development Corporation, 1991, p. 9).

NAS is currently in the scale-up phase of its effort. Its designs are being widely diffused in partnering jurisdictions across the nation. NAS's strategy for scale-up is based on the belief that school transformation can only take place with strong district support. At the beginning of the scale-up phase in 1995, NAS sought to partner with jurisdictions that would commit to five-year partnerships with it and the design teams to create a supportive environment for schoolwide reform. NAS partnered with ten jurisdictions: Cincinnati, Ohio; Miami-Dade County, Florida; several districts in Kentucky; Maryland; Memphis, Tennessee; Pittsburgh, Pennsylvania; Philadelphia, Pennsylvania; San Antonio, Texas; San Diego, California; and several districts in Washington state. All of these jurisdictions insisted that the participating schools meet district or state standards and that students be assessed against district and state mandated tests.

As NAS entered the scale-up phase, seven design teams were involved:

- Audrey Cohen College (AC) (currently renamed Purpose-Centered Education);

- Authentic Teaching, Learning, and Assessment for All Students (AT);

- Co-NECT Schools (Co-NECT);

- Expeditionary Learning/Outward Bound (ELOB);

- Modern Red Schoolhouse (MRSH);

- National Alliance for Restructuring Education (NARE) (currently renamed America's Choice Design Network); and

- Roots & Wings (RW).

While each design has unique features, the designs commonly emphasize school change in the following areas (referred to as elements): organization and governance; teacher professional development; content and performance standards; curriculum and instructional strategies; and parent and community involvement. The focus in this analysis is to examine the relationships among various factors (at the district, school, teacher, classroom, and student levels) and the implementation of designs, classroom practices, and student achievement.

Since RAND's programs of studies began at the beginning of scale-up, NAS's portfolio of teams has changed significantly. For instance, another design—Urban Learning Centers (ULC)—was implementing in the Los Angeles area during the development phase of NAS, but when scale-up began, this design team was not included in the NAS portfolio because the team had not shown the capacity to go to scale. Since that time, ULC has shown this capacity and is currently being marketed by NAS as one of its designs.   Moreover, Audrey Cohen (AC) College did not show the progress during scale-up that NAS desired, and this team was dropped from the portfolio. To date, NAS has ten teams in its portfolio: Accelerated Schools, America's Choice, ATLAS Communities, Co-NECT, ELOB, Leonard Bernstein Center, Modern Red Schoolhouse, Success for All/Roots & Wings, Turning Points, and Urban Learning Centers. Readers can find information on these design teams at http://www.newamericanschools.org/teams.

NAS currently encourages the implementation of comprehensive school approaches in over 3,000 schools by advocating the adoption of designs and assistance from NAS design teams. This count includes all schools in which designs were *ever* implemented including schools that dropped designs or changed to a different design. For example, with the transition of National Alliance to America's Choice, several schools in Kentucky dropped the NARE design and did not switch to America's Choice. These schools are still included in the total count. Moreover, NAS also recently expanded to ten teams, greatly increasing its school count. For example, just by adding Accelerated Schools to its portfolio it added roughly 700 schools. A few years ago, NAS began to count all schools implementing the Success for All (SFA) reading program as part of its portfolio, even though the original intent of NAS was to expand the SFA reading program into other subject areas such as mathematics and social studies, thus becoming Roots & Wings.

RELATIONSHIP OF NAS TO FEDERAL SUPPORT FOR SCHOOLWIDE CHANGE

The purposes and approaches of NAS and its design teams are the same as those of "schoolwide" Title I programs[1] and the Comprehensive School Reform Demonstration (CSRD) program also known as Obey-Porter (see Kirby et al., in review).[2] These two pro-

---

[1]"Schoolwide" programs, available for funding since 1988, allow schools to use Title I money with other dollars to improve school performance as opposed to targeting Title I money solely to qualified students. The 1994 Improving America's Schools Act encourages more wide-range adoption of schoolwide programs (see http://www.ed.gov/legislation/ESEA). Currently, schools can use their Title I funding to improve the entire instructional program throughout the school if at least 50 percent of the students within the school are from poor families. (For a discussion of the 1994 Improving America's Schools Act see U.S. Department of Education, 1993; and Borman et al., 1996).

[2]To further the implementation of comprehensive, whole-school reforms, the CSRD was established in November 1997. In both FY1998 and FY1999, a total of $145 million was appropriated for the CSRD program, to be used to help schools develop comprehensive school reform based on reliable research and effective practices. The majority (83 percent in FY1998 and 77 percent in FY1999) of the funds are committed to Title I schools. Part of the money ($25 million in FY1998 and FY1999) was available to all public schools, including those ineligible for Title I, as part of the Fund for the Improvement in Education (FIE) program. Approximately 1,800 schools received at least $50,000 per year for three years under the CSRD program, beginning in FY1998. There was an increase of $75 million for FY2000 ($50 million in Title I/Section 1502 funds and $25 million in FIE funds) over the $145 million appropriated for FY1998 and FY1999, to allow 1,000 additional schools to undertake comprehensive reform. For FY2000, Congress appropriated $170 million to support comprehensive reforms in schools eligible for Title I funds. An additional $50 million is available to all public schools, including those eligible for Title I. A total of $260 million has been appropriated for the CSRD program for FY2001. These funds became available July 1, 2001. In FY1998, a total of 1,867 schools received CSRD funds. In FY1999 and FY2000, a small number of additional schools received CSRD awards: 62 schools in FY1999 and 103 in FY2000. These schools include schools in the 50 states, the District of Columbia,

grams are targeted to improve the performance of high-poverty schools. Each intends to improve the performance of at-risk students and schools by having schools adopt a unified, coherent approach to reform rather than adding fragmented programs or investing in personnel dedicated to a small group of students in pullout programs. Each model intends to serve all students, not just subgroups of students. Given the similar intentions of NAS and both federal initiatives, findings on its attempts at whole-school change can help inform the needed policy improvement for the many schools that serve low-income students through the Title I and CSRD programs.

PURPOSE AND STUDY QUESTIONS

This study aims to shed light on the policy approach and strategies of the NAS educational reform initiative that incorporates several different whole-school reform designs. Our research focuses on the designs that were implemented in San Antonio, Texas, a district that was viewed during the course of our data collection as having a supportive environment for NAS in terms of educational mission and vision, finance and governance arrangements, and extant policies. This study focuses on the conditions at the district, school, and classroom level that are related to design implementation, changes in classroom instruction, and student achievement. The analyses here offer both useful and provocative insights that can help inform the NAS effort and larger federal efforts to implement comprehensive school reform aimed at improving teaching and learning, particularly in high-poverty settings.

Specifically, this study addresses the following questions:

- Do the NAS designs extend beyond changes in school organization and governance and permeate classrooms? Do NAS teachers and students interact with each other and subject materials in ways that reflect the innovative curricular and instructional approaches of the design teams?

Puerto Rico, and schools administered by the Bureau of Indian Affairs (see Kirby et al., in review; http://www.ed.gov/offices/OESE/compreform).

- What factors at the district, school, and classroom level are related to implementation of designs, changes in classroom instruction, and student achievement?

STUDY DESIGN

During the course of this study, four NAS designs were being implemented in San Antonio—Co-NECT Schools, Expeditionary Learning/
Outward Bound, Modern Red Schoolhouse, and Success for All/
Roots & Wings (see Table 1.1 for a brief description of these designs).
In order to understand how the NAS design teams influenced
teaching and learning across subject areas, we monitored a sample of
fourth grade teachers across these four designs in addition to similar
teachers in non-NAS schools by gathering a variety of data about
classrooms during the 1997–1998 and 1998–1999 school years. In
cooperation with the San Antonio school district, we selected our
sample of teachers from NAS's sites and some comparison sites (i.e.,
schools not implementing any whole-school reform as yet).[3]
Because San Antonio did not want to overburden its schools by
mandating their participation in research activities, the Associate
Superintendent of Curriculum and Instruction sent a letter to all 65
elementary schools in the district requesting their participation in
the RAND study. While not a random sampling process, which is not
feasible given the self-selection of designs by schools and the limited
number of schools implementing designs, district staff assisted
RAND in selecting teachers that were representative of the elementary schools in the district (e.g., representative in terms of academic
performance and school demographic characteristics).

We also relied on information from surveys of teachers and principals, student achievement and background characteristics, observations and classroom artifacts, and interviews with district staff to
help us address the questions of this study.

---

[3]At the time of this study, the San Antonio superintendent had a stated goal of all the
schools in the district adopting some type of whole-school reform design (NAS or non-
NAS designs) by fall 1999.

Table 1.1

NAS Designs in San Antonio

Co-NECT Schools (Co-NECT)

Co-NECT emphasizes three important components in its design: an interdisciplinary project-based curriculum; integrated technology; and continuous assessment of school and student progress. The design draws from research supporting authentic pedagogy to advocate its approach to student learning. Co-NECT maintains that higher-order thinking skills are best developed through projects that apply multiple content area skills and knowledge to address real-life problems. Modern technology, featuring desktop Internet participation, allows students to perform online research, communicate with students in other schools, and contact experts in their project field. Co-NECT expects school staff to focus on results by using multiple forms of assessments and tools to monitor progress, including portfolios, culminating project demonstrations, and other types of measures in addition to the local standardized tests. Co-NECT encourages reorganization of schools into small communities of teachers and students, characterized by teachers collaborating during common planning time and individual teachers staying with a class of students for two to three years. To support the design, each small group of schools within a region receives training and guidance from a Co-NECT site director and has access to online resources for developing project-based curriculum.

Expeditionary Learning/Outward Bound (ELOB)

ELOB believes that students learn best when curriculum and instruction are transformed into expeditions of learning that develop their intellectual, physical, and civic skills. Expeditions are multidisciplinary but focus on a single theme, and they typically involve service and fieldwork and culminate in a student presentation that is measured by student-defined rubrics. The design is based on the Outward Bound program, which also emphasizes the importance of reflection and critique, community, and collaboration. The design requires that the schedule and instruction be organized around the expedition rather than subject periods and calls for teachers to plan together once a week. ELOB also encourages teachers to stay with a class of students for at least two years.

Modern Red Schoolhouse (MRSH)

MRSH blends elements of traditional education with new instructional methods to provide all students with a strong foundation in American culture as well as skills needed for future employment. The design embraces standards-based reform and assessment. It works with schools to set high expectations around state and local standards and to map out an instructional program that will allow students to attain the

Table 1.1 (continued)

established goals. MRSH encourages adoption of the Core Knowledge scope and sequence and locally trains teachers how to develop curricula that are tied to the standards and are coherent across grade levels. Teachers are encouraged to adapt instructional strategies to meet the needs of individual learners and to utilize individual
student contracts to assess progress as measured by tests and performance on
teacher-developed capstone units.

Success For All / Roots & Wings (SFA/RW)

SFA is the reading component of the RW comprehensive model, and was the only
component of RW being implemented in the schools we studied. SFA is targeted at
ensuring that all students succeed in reading, particularly in urban schools. To this
end, the program attempts to decrease low achievement, special education referrals,
and attendance problems. SFA uses a highly structured curriculum based on research
about effective practice. Students are homogeneously grouped by ability throughout
the school for the first 90 minutes of a school day. Within the 90-minute block, teachers are required to use design materials, including basal readers, anthologies, novels,
and student workbooks to teach scripted lessons. The design embeds formal assessments into the curriculum at least every eight weeks to assess progress and reassign
students if needed. SFA calls for a full-time facilitator to assist teachers in implementation of the program and additional staff to provide tutoring and organize materials.

UNDERSTANDING THE RELATIONSHIPS AMONG NAS DESIGNS, CLASSROOM INSTRUCTION, AND STUDENT ACHIEVEMENT

While NAS aims to help schools and districts significantly raise the
achievement of large numbers of students through design-based assistance, improving student and school performance is a critical goal
of all comprehensive school reforms.

To understand the relative impact of NAS designs (and comprehensive school reform models), we need to address a variety of factors
throughout the educational system. No doubt, the process of school
change to improve student achievement is complex and difficult. It
requires the coordination of a variety of actors and factors to make it
work. The framework portrayed in Figure 1.1 portrays some of that
complexity. In our other research on NAS, we have highlighted those
conditions that are related to implementation of NAS designs at the
school level (Bodilly, 1998, 2001; Berends, 2000; Berends and Kirby et
al., 2001; Kirby, Berends, and Naftel, 2001). In this report, we focus
on those factors at the district, school, classroom, and student levels

RAND*MR1483-1.1*

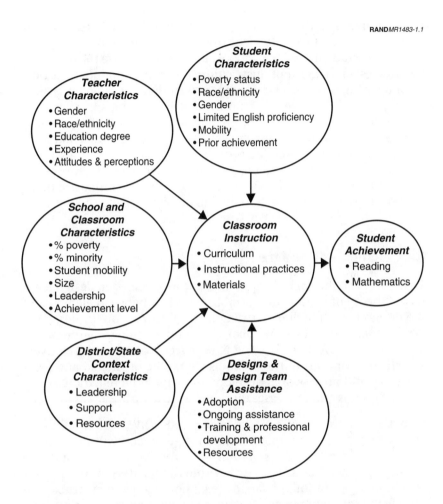

**Figure 1.1—A Conceptual Framework for Understanding the Relationships
Among NAS Designs, Classroom Instruction,
and Student Achievement**

that are related to changes in classroom instruction and student achievement scores.

The overarching concept underlying NAS is the development of an intervention by external change agents who provide assistance during the implementation process in order to improve schools and student outcomes. Even after controlling for other important contexts—e.g., student, teacher, school, and district—these relationships among designs, classroom instruction, and achievement are critical for improving schools, classrooms, and student learning: a critical assumption of NAS itself. Certainly, the relationships in Figure 1.1 can be portrayed in a much more complex manner with additional arrows in multiple directions, suggesting a myriad of direct and indirect effects. However, the focus of this report is on those classroom practices promoted by NAS designs and influenced by factors at the district and school levels. Figure 1.1 is intended to emphasize those relationships, some of which we highlight further in the sections that follow.

Core Elements of Designs

To accomplish the goal of improving performance, each design team has a "theory of action" that establishes a link between elements of the design (which include curriculum and instruction, professional development, school governance), classroom learning environments, and student performance. The NAS designs range from relatively specific descriptions of how schools should be organized and what materials and professional development should be relied on to less specific visions and processes for school restructuring.

One of the more specific NAS designs is SFA/RW, which builds on years of research and implementation experiences with the reading and writing program *Success for All*. SFA/RW provides an abundance of print materials, assessments, professional development, and specified organizational changes (e.g., homogeneous instructional groups that are reorganized frequently to address students' needs). The design begins implementation with a specific focus on changing curriculum and instruction.

In contrast, some of the other NAS designs are more process oriented. For instance, ELOB is less structured than SFA/RW and is based on design principles that reflect the design's origins in the Outward Bound program. Students' experiences in ELOB schools consist primarily of engaging in multidisciplinary, project-based learning expeditions that include intellectual, service, and physical dimensions. Teachers play a critical role in developing the expeditions, which involve a great deal of effort and imagination.

Thus, it is important to remember the unique attributes of each design in terms of its complexity and specificity, elements of schooling emphasized, and the different strategies for implementation. Certainly, we cannot capture all of the uniqueness of each design in the current analysis. For further elaboration, we suggest looking at RAND's other NAS studies that have pointed to these characteristics and the importance of looking at changes in designs over time (see Bodilly, 2001; Berends and Kirby et al., 2001; Kirby et al., 2001; Berends, 1999, 2000; Glennan, 1998).

Student Characteristics

An important set of factors that affect implementation of school restructuring efforts and their effects is student background (e.g., socioeconomic status or poverty level, race-ethnicity, gender, English language proficiency, and mobility) and prior achievement. Within school reform efforts, it is important to understand how changes in schooling activities are related to students' social background characteristics, their home environments, mobility patterns between schools, and their preexisting levels of academic achievement in school (Berends et al., 1999; Koretz, 1996; Meyer, 1996). Policymakers focus on manipulating the "lever" at the school level to improve learning opportunities and performance. Yet, when assessing the impact of NAS and its designs on classroom instruction, it is important to understand the net influence of school reform activities, especially with the number of studies that have shown the importance of student background in the learning process (see Coleman et al., 1966; Jencks et al., 1972; Gamoran, 1987, 1992; Bryk et al., 1993). That is, when assessing the effects of classroom environments, we need to consider other important school, classroom, and student factors, and control for them when appropriate.

Teacher Characteristics

Without willing and able teachers who embrace reform and provide the necessary leadership to undertake it, no change can be enacted, no matter how effective it may be. Teachers are the "street-level bureaucrats" at the core of educational change (Weatherly and Lipsky, 1977) and as Fullan succinctly stated, educational reform depends on "what teachers do and think—it's as simple and as complex as that" (Fullan, 2001, p. 115).

Educators must respond to multiple, simultaneous pressures and demands. For many teachers, policy goals and activities are simply part of a broader environment that presses in upon their classrooms. Their ability to cope with these demands, and their commitment to change are crucial to coherent and sustained implementation. Moreover, engagement in reforms may be affected by teachers' personal characteristics, such as their age and experience (Huberman, 1989), gender (Datnow, 1998, 2000a), and race (Foster, 1993), but not necessarily correlated (Berends, 2000; Datnow and Castellano, 2000), so it remains important to examine these characteristics for the specific reforms under consideration (Berends and Kirby et al., 2001; Kirby et al., 2001). Thus, teachers matter: Their experience, subject-based expertise, attitudes, and orientations are important in determining the degree and level of implementation.

In short, teachers are central to all organizational changes that alter student-teacher interactions occurring in classrooms to improve student learning (Gamoran et al., 1995; Oakes et al., 1992). Over time, teachers carry with them a great deal of knowledge based on their educational attainment, teaching experience, and other personal characteristics that together are likely related to their engagement in schoolwide restructuring activities (Louis and Marks, 1998). Thus, it is important to examine the relationships among various teacher background characteristics, classroom instruction, and student achievement.

School and Classroom Characteristics

Characteristics of schools and classrooms are also likely to influence the adoption of schoolwide designs and their effects on classrooms and students. In our work, we examine whether school and classroom characteristics such as the minority and poverty composition are related to implementation and performance (Berends and Kirby et al., 2001; Berends, 1999, 2000).

Schools and classrooms that face challenges in terms of poverty may encounter difficulties with restructuring efforts such as whole-school designs because high-poverty schools may lack the necessary resources to provide a quality education (Lippman et al., 1996), because students may have lower levels of engagement, effort, and aspirations (Hoffer, 1992; Ralph, 1990; Fordham and Ogbu, 1986), and because teachers may not have the necessary supports they need to foster collaborative relationships necessary for school improvement efforts (Hoffer, 1992; see also Berends and Kirby et al., 2001; Berends and King, 1994).

However, because federal funding such as Title I is oriented toward disadvantaged students and schools, the effects of socioeconomic and minority composition are likely to be mediated by the effect of increased resources. In fact, since the 1994 reauthorization of Title I, schools with more than half of their students eligible for free or reduced price lunch may use Title I funds for schoolwide programs. Thus, there may be a positive relationship between high-poverty schools and schoolwide implementations such as NAS designs because of such funding sources.

District/State Context

Research also underscores the importance of the external environment in the process of change, especially district and state support and stability of leadership (Fullan, 2001; Datnow, 2000b; Bodilly and Berends, 1999; Yonezawa and Datnow, 1999; Bodilly, 1998; Glennan, 1998). Districts and states can facilitate and foster change by providing resources for the school and for professional staff development, and by showing active support for schools implementing designs.

The federal and state policy context is likely to play a role in implementing schoolwide reform (Fullan, 2001; Koretz and Barron, 1998). For example, the recent CSRD program directly supports design-based reforms such as NAS by providing at least $50,000 to schools to pay for the related services. Some states and districts with high-stakes accountability systems may force low-performing schools to adopt designs. They may also facilitate a more effective matching process for schools to select designs based on their local needs (see Bodilly and Berends, 1999; Bodilly, 1998; Smith et al., 1996).

Bodilly (1998) found that districts play a strong role in determining the initial and sustained viability of the relationship between the school and the design team. Early on in the scale-up phase, many schools' staff members complain about the district's poor planning and scanty provision of time to make decisions, issues brought up in other assessments of the adoption of schoolwide programs (Desimone, 2000; Wong and Meyer, 1998).

RAND's prior case studies (see Bodilly, 1998; Bodilly and Berends, 1999) reveal that higher average levels of implementation are found in districts where there is stable district leadership, a high priority placed on the effort, a lack of major budget crisis or other crises, and a history of trust between the central office and the schools. School-level respondents directly link these factors to greater efforts at implementation. When these factors are missing, school respondents report that their own efforts stall or are less intense.

While political support from the district is crucial for design implementation, its attention can be buttressed by significant changes in regulatory and financial practices. Schools attempting comprehensive school reform to address their particular problems can be supported through increased site-level control over their curriculum and instruction, their budgets, their positions and staffing, and most essentially their mission. Comprehensive school reform is not confined to the adoption of a new mandated curriculum or a few new instructional strategies. Instead, it may require rethinking and adoption at the school level of new curriculum and instructional approaches and the accompanying professional development. District flexibility in allowing schools to pursue this rethinking is a critical aspect for design-based schools. Development and implementation of such curriculum and instructional strategies at the school level may be significantly hampered without district support through resource allocation for instructional positions, materials, technology, professional development, etc.

In short, the district-level politics, policies, and practices may promote or derail schoolwide reform efforts such as the NAS designs. In fact, schools may look to district leadership, climate, and regulations to understand if it is worth their time and effort to invest in transforming.

External Assistance by Design Teams

How schools go about selecting a design has implications for the implementation that follows (Datnow and Stringfield, 2000; Desimone, 2000; Bodilly, 1998; Consortium for Policy Research in Education, 1998; Smith et al., 1998; Stringfield, 1998; Ross et al., 1997). For example, if a school is forced to adopt a design, it is not surprising that teachers resist engaging in its activities. Yet, some schools are often targets for forced restructuring efforts, particularly those schools that exhibit chronic poor performance. Thus, a critical aim of the NAS designs before implementation even begins is to obtain the buy-in of teachers for the planned restructuring activities. Most of the designs require between 75 and 80 percent of the teachers voting in favor of the designs. The rationale is that if the vast majority of the staff votes to adopt the design, they will commit to making the changes necessary during the implementation process.

Clear communication by designs to schools is critical for not only the selection of any one design, but also its implementation—something that external assistance providers have found challenging when attempting to help a large number of schools (Bodilly, 1998). Communication to schools during both the selection and implementation processes can take several different forms, including design fairs, print materials, use of computer software and the Internet, workshops, retreats, school visits, and site-based facilitators. For instance, school visits by design team staff on a regular basis to help teachers address issues related to developing curriculum units or the use of rubrics to assess students is intended to help teachers implement project-based learning and the assessment of that learning within the context of the design. Other types of communication might be effective as well, and the clearer and more consistent the information provided about implementation by designs to schools, the smoother the implementation process is likely to be.

For implementation of any program, resources are critical (Keltner, 1998; McLaughlin, 1990). It is a common finding that when resources decrease or disappear, the implementation is likely to diminish (Glennan, 1998; Montjoy and O'Toole, 1979). If teachers receive needed funds, professional development from design teams for de-sign implementation, materials to support implementation, and the time to plan and develop their programs, it is likely that implemen-tation will deepen over time.

By gathering information about different aspects of the system from the district to teachers and students in schools, we hope to shed light on how the NAS initiative is unfolding in terms of implementation and outcomes in a high-poverty, low-performing district in a high-stakes accountability environment. While facing many challenges, this district was inviting and provided significant resources to schools implementing NAS designs.

ORGANIZATION OF REPORT

Chapter Two provides details of the RAND sample of NAS schools and classrooms analyzed for this study, and presents a profile of these schools and classrooms in terms of their student and teacher demographics. Chapter Three places NAS design implementation within the context of a high-poverty district. We describe various as-pects of the district environment in which designs were imple-mented and discuss the implications for comprehensive school reform.

Chapter Four presents results from a variety of data sources (e.g., teacher surveys, classroom observations, interviews, and classroom artifacts) that describe school organization, adoption and support of the NAS designs, and teachers' training and professional develop-ment in NAS and non-NAS schools. In Chapter Five, we draw on similar data to describe the instructional activities in NAS and non-NAS classrooms. Chapter Six examines the relationship between in-structional activities and student achievement, controlling for other factors. Finally, Chapter Seven discusses the policy implications of our results.

Chapter Two

SOURCES OF DATA

Fifteen public school districts serve more than 200,000 students living in the city of San Antonio and surrounding communities. The San Antonio district that we studied is the second largest district in the county and the seventh largest in the state. Most of the approximately 60,000 students who attend schools in San Antonio live within the city limits, and the district has the highest proportion of students who are eligible for free or reduced price lunch in the county.[1] Most students in the district are Hispanic (85 percent); the second largest group (10 percent) is African American. Approximately 16 percent of students in the district are classified as Limited English Proficient. Since 1994, the proportion of San Antonio students failing to earn passing rates on the Texas Assessment of Academic Skills (TAAS) in each school year has consistently been the highest or second highest in the county.

It is within this context of high-poverty and low student performance that elementary schools in San Antonio began the process of adopting NAS reform models. Of the 64 elementary schools in the district, three schools began implementation during the 1995–1996 school year, nine schools the following year, and 20 schools during the 1997–1998 school year. By the 1998–1999 school year, 39 of 64 elementary schools in the district had adopted NAS designs. Table 2.1 lists the number of schools adopting specific designs in each year.

---

[1]For more information see http://www.saisd.net and Texas Education Agency web page http://www.tea.state.tx.us.

Table 2.1

Elementary Schools Adopting NAS Designs in San Antonio by Year

	Number of Schools				
	1995–1996	1996–1997	1997–1998	1998–1999	Totals
Co-NECT			3	1	4
ELOB	1	2			3
MRSH		5	4	1	10
SFA/RW	2	2	13	5	22
NAS Total	3	9	20	7	39

RAND collected data on a sample of fourth grade teachers and their students during two school years, 1997–1998 and 1998–1999 (see Tables 2.2 and 2.3). Fourth grade was an advantageous selection for several reasons: most NAS designs were being implemented in elementary schools; the state administered its test to students in the third grade, providing a baseline for test score analysis; and teacher questionnaire items were already developed and tested with fourth grade teachers. In addition, the school district expressed its preference for a fourth grade focus.

Table 2.2

Target Sample of Schools Compared with Final Study Sample
by Type of Data Collection and NAS Design Team

	Requested to Participate	Returned Teacher Surveys	Returned Principal Surveys	Returned Stanford-9 Testing	Classroom Observations
Number of Schools in 1997–1998 School Year					
Co-NECT	2	2	2	2	1
ELOB	2	2	1	1	1
MRSH	4	4	4	4	2
SFA/RW	8	8	8	9	1
Non-NAS	10	8	9	10	2
Total	26	24	24	26	7
Number of Schools in 1998–1999 School Year					
Co-NECT	2	2	2	2	2
ELOB	2	2	1	2	2
MRSH	4	4	2	4	2
SFA/RW	8	8	7	8	2
Non-NAS	7	7	7	7	2
Total	23	23	19	23	10

Table 2.3

**Target Sample of Teachers Compared with Final Study Sample
by Type of Data Collection and NAS Design Team**

	Requested to Participate	Returned Teacher Surveys	Returned Surveys & Stanford-9 Testing	Observations
Number of Teachers in 1997–1998 School Year				
Co-NECT	6	6	6	3
ELOB	4	4	2	2
MRSH	12	10	10	3
SFA/RW	26	23	22	2
Non-NAS	26	23	23	2
Total	74	66	63	12
Number of Teachers in 1998–1999 School Year				
Co-NECT	11	11	10	4
ELOB	8	8	6	5
MRSH	13	13	11	3
SFA/RW	32	32	27	4
Non-NAS	19	19	19	3
Total	83	83	73	19

Generally, in each school year we were able to gather teacher survey data and supplemental student test scores in reading (Stanford-9), including over 850 students in over 60 classrooms in over 20 schools. Moreover, during the course of this study, we were able to obtain information on all the teachers and students in the district to provide a benchmark for the analyses reported here. In 1997–1998, we were also able to observe and gather classroom artifacts from 12 teachers in NAS and non-NAS schools. In the following year, we gathered such data from 19 teachers. Each of these data collection efforts is described more fully in the sections that follow.

The assistant superintendent's office demonstrated its support for our study by asking principals to announce the study to their staff and to invite all fourth grade teachers to participate in the study. Once the initial volunteers were reported, RAND attempted to balance the representation of designs in the sample by approaching schools of underrepresented designs. While the RAND sample of NAS and non-NAS schools cannot be considered random, district staff indicated that the schools selected were typical of elementary schools in the district. Comparisons of demographic and other characteristics for students (i.e., gender, race, Limited English Proficient, special education status, average test scores, and mobility rates) and teachers (i.e., gender, race, highest degree earned, years of teaching experience) indicated no significant differences, on average, between the RAND sample and district populations. Each selected teacher was asked to administer the Stanford-9 to his or her fourth grade students and to complete a teacher survey. Teacher focus groups were conducted in eight schools during the 1997–1998 school year. A subset of teachers agreed to provide classroom logs and samples of student work, and allowed classroom observations once in the spring of the 1997–1998 school year and three times in the 1998–1999 school year. In addition, principals in the sample schools were asked to complete a telephone interview, during which a survey was completed. A brief description of these data collection efforts follows (see Table 2.4).

TEACHER DATA

In late spring of the 1997–1998 school year, with the help of district staff, we contacted 74 teachers in 26 schools to participate. Three of the schools refused to participate. Of those 74 teachers initially contacted, 63 teachers in 23 schools agreed to participate, returned completed teacher surveys, and their students completed the Stanford-9 reading test resulting in an 85 percent response rate for teachers and classes with student achievement scores.

In 1998–1999, we returned to the 23 schools that participated in our study the previous year. Because we wanted to increase our sample of teachers, we contacted 83 teachers in these 23 schools. Of those contacted, we received completed teacher surveys and Stanford-9 tests from 73 teachers (88 percent). Between the spring of 1998 and 1999, one of our sampled schools went from having no design in place to adopting SFA/RW.

Not all teachers had complete survey data across both years, given that different teachers were included in both years. Thus, for the longitudinal descriptions of NAS and non-NAS classrooms, we tracked indicators for the 40 teachers for whom we had complete data from both the 1997–1998 and 1998–1999 school years (see Table 2.5). In addition to these teacher data from RAND surveys, we also obtained information on teachers from the district, such as demographic

Table 2.4

RAND Classroom Study in San Antonio Data Collection

Type of Data	Information Provided
Teacher survey	• Design team program characteristics • Instructional strategies • Professional development activities • Teacher background • Classroom climate and other characteristics
Teacher logs of classroom activities	• Design team program characteristics • Instructional strategies
Observations of classroom instruction	• Design team program characteristics • Instructional strategies
Teacher interviews & focus groups	• Design team program characteristics • Instructional strategies • Design team implementation benchmarks • Professional development activities • Common planning time • Resources for implementation
Principal & instructional guide interviews	• NAS design implementation • School climate and other characteristics • Professional development activities • Resources for implementation
Design team interviews	• Design team program characteristics • Instructional strategies • Design team implementation benchmarks • NAS design implementation • Professional development activities • Resources for implementation
District interviews	• NAS design implementation • Professional development activities • District policies • Resources for implementation
Student characteristics and performance	• TAAS mathematics, reading, and writing scores at student and item level (linked to teachers and schools) • Stanford Open-Ended Reading Achievement Test 9th Edition at student and item level (linked to teachers and schools) • Demographic and individual characteristics of students

Table 2.5

Longitudinal Sample of Teachers in NAS and Non-NAS Schools, 1997–1998
and 1998–1999 School Years

	Co-NECT	ELOB	MRSH	SFA/RW	Non-NAS	Totals
Number of schools	2	2	3	6	7	20
Number of teachers	4	3	8	11	14	40

NOTE: Teachers who completed the survey in both spring 1998 and spring 1999 and who were in the same school, same design, and teaching fourth grade in both years.

characteristics (race-ethnicity and gender), years of experience, and highest degree obtained.

We discuss the results from this longitudinal sample of teachers in Chapters Four and Five. We limit our discussion to this longitudinal sample of 40 fourth grade teachers who completed surveys in both the spring of 1998 and 1999 and remained in the same school/ design/teaching assignment. We do this because for this study our interest lay in examining what changes, if any, occurred during the early stages of implementation in school organization, teachers' professional work lives, and their classroom instruction.

We also compiled survey results from the larger sample (66 teachers in 1998 and 83 in 1999). A comparison of average response rates found few differences between the two samples. A detailed analysis of individual teacher responses found no substantive differences between these larger samples and what we find in the longitudinal teacher sample of 40 teachers.

Because of the small size of the longitudinal sample analyzed, we do not focus much attention on testing the statistically significant differences between NAS and non-NAS teachers. Given the design, most standard statistical tests comparing the 40 NAS and non-NAS teachers in the longitudinal sample would fail to detect many real differences. However, in conjunction with the qualitative data from this study, the NAS and non-NAS comparisons shed light on a variety of factors related to implementing NAS designs in a high-poverty urban district.

Surveys

The teacher survey fielded during the spring 1998 semester and then again in spring 1999 was designed to provide a broad measure of instructional practices in NAS and non-NAS classrooms. Teachers were asked to report on a range of instructional strategies, some of which reflected a focus on basic skills and tended toward more conventional practices, and others of which reflected more reform-like methods. Given that the NAS designs emphasize changes in instructional conditions whether through building basic skills and then higher-order thinking (e.g., SFA/RW) or through theme-based projects that last for several weeks (e.g., Co-NECT or ELOB) (see Bodilly, 2001), we would expect the implementation of designs to result in changes in teaching strategies.

General topics covered in the survey include school and classroom characteristics, instructional strategies and materials, skills and assessments emphasized, resources, parent involvement and community relations, impact of design team and reform efforts, professional development, and perceptions and attitudes toward teaching.

Two versions of the survey were fielded in each year, one to fourth grade teachers in a sample of schools adopting NAS designs, the other to fourth grade teachers in non-NAS schools. The two forms of the surveys varied only slightly. For instance, three items specifically related to the implementation of NAS designs were not included in the survey received by non-NAS teachers. A few items in other sections also referred specifically to NAS designs. On the non-NAS version, these items were either omitted or had slightly different wording (e.g., whereas NAS teachers were asked about the NAS design being implemented in their school, non-NAS teachers were asked about the school reform efforts in their district). For example, an item on the NAS version that asked if an activity was "specifically oriented toward the design team program activities" was changed to "specifically oriented toward the reform efforts of San Antonio" on the non-NAS version.

These surveys were developed in conjunction with RAND's ongoing case study work (Bodilly, 1998). As part of our overall survey development, we conducted phone interviews with design team representatives about what specific indicators and events would be observed in design-based classrooms. For the survey development, we also relied on other studies that have examined instruction with surveys (Newmann et al., 1996; Gamoran et al., 1995; Burstein et al., 1995; Porter, 1995; Porter and Smithson, 1995; Porter et al., 1993; see also Mayer, 1999).

Longitudinal Sample of 40 Teachers Compared with Elementary Teachers in District

Overall, it appears that in demographic terms, the longitudinal survey sample of 40 teachers was a fairly representative group of teachers within the school district. There were few differences when comparing teachers in our sample to all fourth grade teachers in the San Antonio school district (Table 2.6). Teachers in this sample and the district as a whole were similar with respect to gender, racial-ethnic characteristics, and average years of experience.   Whereas 40 percent of teachers in the district had earned master's degrees, 45 percent of the teachers in the longitudinal sample had attained this level of education.

Table 2.6

Teacher Characteristics—District-Wide vs. RAND Survey Sample, 1997–1998 School Year

	District (n = 329)	Survey Sample (n = 40)
Male	11%	8%
With MA degrees	40%	45%
Average years' teaching experience	13	13
White	37%	33%
African American	15%	20%
Latino/Latina	47%	47%
Asian American	0.3%	None
Native American	0.3%	None

Observations and Logs of Instructional Activities[2]

In the spring of the 1997–1998 school year, RAND conducted class-room observations of a subsample of 12 teachers from the larger group of 64. These observations consisted of a RAND researcher shadowing a teacher for a day, writing detailed summaries of class-room activities, taking notes on the general description of the class-room and the resources in it, and informally discussing design team activities with the teacher.

School observations first began in the spring of 1998 and continued throughout the 1998–1999 school year. Observations, targeting the fourth grade level, covered ten different schools. Data were collected in two Co-NECT, two ELOB, two MRSH, two SFA/RW, and two non-NAS schools. In the first year of our study, in addition to observations, we aimed to gather more extensive classroom data through (1) teacher logs of assignments, homework, projects, quizzes/tests/exams, and papers or reports over a five-week period, and (2) illustrative teacher-selected samples of student work related to a major project assigned during the spring semester. Because we could not gain entrée into these classrooms until May, right after the administration of TAAS, and because our logs were overly bur-densome, the response rate for these 12 teachers was less than desir-able. Five of 12 teachers (42 percent) returned completed logs.

Therefore in the second year, we significantly revamped our data collection methods for observations and logs of instructional activi-ties. Teachers were not asked to submit logs of assignments. Rather, arrangements were made to observe 19 teachers across ten different schools—two Co-NECT, two ELOB, two MRSH, two SFA/RW, and two non-NAS schools—on three separate occasions. Moreover, a staff person on site in San Antonio interviewed them at length over the course of one school year. In addition, teachers provided work assignments, lesson plans, and even district memos when appropriate.

---

[2]Each teacher who participated in this part of the study received a $200 honorarium.

Interviews

In the spring of 1998, we conducted focus group interviews with fourth grade teachers from eight different schools, including schools implementing each of the four NAS designs and some comparison schools. Our aim was to get a representation of teachers within NAS schools to provide information about what activities were undertaken across grade levels. These interviews were conducted to help us better understand design team program characteristics, the nature of instructional strategies, the variety of professional development activities, and the types of available classroom-level resources. Additional information about these schools, professional development activities, and the resources available for design implementation was provided by 45-minute structured interviews with principals.

During the 1998–1999 school year, after each observation, teachers were interviewed about what occurred during the observation as well as about other more general issues having to do with design implementation, instructional strategies, professional development, and other matters related to design and district initiatives.

In addition, we conducted interviews of NAS design team leaders, district staff, school instructional leaders, and principals.

STUDENT DATA

Data for individual students were obtained mainly through the cooperation of the central office staff, who provided district files on students to RAND for analysis.

Student Achievement

In this study, student achievement was measured in a variety of ways. First, we asked teachers to administer the Stanford-9 open-ended reading test. We decided to use the Stanford-9 because, as a commercial test that could be nationally normed, it differed somewhat from conventional multiple-choice tests. The Stanford-9 test requires students to use an open-ended response format. The test takes about 50 minutes to administer.

In addition, RAND obtained the TAAS mathematics and reading scores for all of the district's third, fourth, and fifth grade students during the time of this study. Our focus was mainly on the 1997–1998 fourth grade cohort. Not only did we track their achievement back to when they were third graders, but we also obtained their scores from the fifth grade to examine achievement growth. Specifically, we analyzed the TAAS mathematics and reading Texas Learning Indices (TLI). These data were linked to teachers and schools in our survey sample. They allowed us to examine achievement across schools and classrooms for the entire district in addition to the RAND sample that included teacher surveys and Stanford-9 tests.

Student Characteristics

Other information available for individual students from district data files included student race-ethnicity, sex, date of birth, poverty status (economically disadvantaged or not), number of weeks the student was in the school during the academic year, limited English proficiency status, and participation in special education or gifted and talented programs.

Examples of Student Work

The teachers we observed in the 1998–1999 school year were asked to provide examples of students' work. We randomly selected a quarter of the students in each class every three months. Once a student was selected, his or her name was removed from the class roster. While no criteria were established with regard to what was submitted, we asked teachers to provide examples of typical work assignments that students produced.

We cannot claim that the submitted work was representative of all student assignments made by a given teacher. However, these examples did provide a glimpse of the types of activities assigned by each of the teachers in our sample.

CAVEAT

District staff assisted RAND in selecting teachers academically and demographically representative of its elementary schools. In light of this sample selection, our findings must be interpreted with care. The small number of schools inspires caution as does the even smaller percentage of teachers observed and interviewed. Confidence in the generalizations, however, lies in the fact that we were able to compare some of our results with the teachers and students in all district schools. Because we were able to draw on a variety of qualitative and quantitative data, we were able to compare findings from these data sources to check the robustness of the findings reported.

In addition to the teacher surveys, test scores, and other quantitative data, our multiple classroom observations, conversations with teachers and school administrators, examination of lesson plans, and analysis of student work revealed that design implementation is greatly affected by the environments of the district and the schools. As will be revealed in detail, the designs themselves were but one means brought in by the district to reform its academically troubled school system.

THE DISTRICT CONTEXT FOR IMPLEMENTATION OF NEW AMERICAN SCHOOLS' DESIGNS IN SAN ANTONIO

While NAS was busy starting up in July of 1991, the San Antonio school district struggled to raise its students' achievement levels and meet the challenges it faced. Given its size of 94 schools, 58,000 students, and 3,800 teachers at the time, productive communication proved problematic as did the effective utilization of district staff. Much energy was expended on the management of day-to-day organizational affairs. According to several central office administrators, instructional practice was too often last addressed. In the words of one, "The school district was perceived as backwater, low performing, not doing anything, in decay."

In November of 1993, the superintendent of San Antonio announced his retirement plans, resulting in an active search for his replacement. The search committee agreed to look for a leader focused on instruction. The academic situation in the district was dire. Forty-six schools within San Antonio were deemed "low performing" according to results on the TAAS, a criterion-referenced test covering different subject areas (particularly reading and mathematics) introduced by the state in the fall of 1990.[1]

The search for San Antonio's new superintendent was narrowed down to a pool of several candidates. The winning candidate was

---

[1]See http://www.tea.state.tx.us/student.assessment/.

hired by the school board on a vote of 4 to 3. From the start, the new superintendent faced tenuous support.

DISTRICT CONTEXT BEFORE THE NEW, REFORM-MINDED SUPERINTENDENT

In what follows, we describe the district context before the new superintendent's arrival in terms of instructional leadership, curriculum and development, professional development, and parent and community involvement.

Instructional Leadership

The focus of the administration prior to the new superintendent's arrival had less to do with issues instructional in nature than managerial and administrational. According to one district administrator, "In previous years, the important thing was, have we got all the kids in place? We're taking care of our problems, fighting all the fires. Are we spending money the right way? Those were the kinds of things we checked on."

In the past, the organization of the central office itself in fact took away from staffs' ability to focus on instructional concerns and to provide schools with necessary assistance.

> All the elementary principals, 65 of them, reported to one person. He evaluated every one and listened to the parent complaints from all 65. The other assistant superintendent was in charge of all the middle and high schools, evaluated every principal and listened to all the complaints. And then they had attached to them, elementary curriculum and instruction and secondary curriculum and instruction [respectively]. . . . What took precedence was keeping schools running.

The assignment of responsibilities within the central office was not designed to foster communication among other staff either, thus making it difficult for them to collaborate with one another. Different central office personnel were responsible for the various programs in place at the time (e.g., Cooperative Learning, New Jersey Writing Style, Reading Styles, and Visual Math).

The comments made by several central staff members who worked in the administration prior to the new superintendent's arrival portrayed the image of a disjointed system, where employees worked hard and did their best in isolation.

> The area superintendents were doing everything. They were doing curriculum, instruction, personnel things in the school, I mean, it was crazy.

> I think the academic support team members were tremendously underutilized. Instead of working on curriculum, they each had a specialty. Like one did cooperative learning, one did learning styles, one did reading styles. They each had these little areas of specialization. . . . No focus. No direction. Just piecemeal.

> The central office people had a frustration about the inability to meet the needs of everybody in the organization in their narrow field that they were working . . .

Within schools, teachers did not necessarily turn to one another for assistance given that they engaged in a variety of programs. The principals, too, were of little help in the area of instruction. Their focus tended to be school operations. According to a central office administrator, the principals pre-1994 were "brought in and bred as managers. The message they heard was manage things well. They were not instructional leaders."

Curriculum and Instruction

Prior to the new superintendent's arrival there was no sense of a unified curricular vision across the district, let alone among the various feeder schools. Individual schools had in place a wide variety of curricular and instructional programs, with little coherence among them. According to one central staff member, "We had a curriculum that really wasn't going anywhere. People weren't using it." When school staff were asked what instructional strategies were in place, a typical response tended to include 12 to 14 different programs. Classrooms basically functioned in isolation. Though people at the district level were responsible for the various programs, there was no expectation for entire schools or even a majority of classrooms to adopt them.

This diversity and range of programs across school campuses made it difficult to know what students were being taught and how learning was being assessed within classrooms across the district. Moreover, without a unified curricular trajectory, the same topics were at times observed being taught at a variety of grade levels. According to one central office staff member:

> We had a lot of redundancy in the curriculum and we had a total lack of direction, in part because each school in this district very much did its own thing. . . . I walked (through) a third, a fifth, a seventh, and a ninth grade classroom. Within the same ten-day period they were all doing the solar system . . . everybody was doing exactly the same thing. The mobiles were hanging in every room. . . . The test was the same.

Professional Development

In addition to minimal instructional leadership and a weak curricular vision, the professional development prior to the new superintendent's arrival was limited, according to central staff members who experienced the leadership of both the old and new superintendents. The district did its best to meet the state's yearly staff development requirements. However, it had no good system of tracking professional development. Moreover, the state did not ask for specific information. Thus, the central office did not develop a coherent strategy for professional development.

Money was spent on upgrading the knowledge and skills of teachers, but "it was the one shot deal with no real follow-up in the classroom or in the school," according to a district staff member. Central office staff reported that the training they provided tended not to be utilized at the school level: "There was a whole lot of training that was happening that was wasted. People would go off, learn something about something, come back to their schools, and not use it." Additionally, administrators at the central office recognized that although some of the professional development they provided served to deepen educators' understanding of specific subjects, they were tied to larger issues such as state standards or student achievement. In the words of a district administrator:

> In 1991, what the central office was about doing was developing teachers' ability to use a curriculum, rather than actually developing the curriculum itself. So it became a lot of instructional strategy development at that point in time. . . . We started doing some things that were about cooperative learning strategies and learning styles and much more about techniques—how to teach much more than what to teach. And since there was no professional development function other than that, that became really more of a professional development function.

Parent and Community Involvement

As for school interaction with parents and the community at large, that too was problematic. According to a central office administrator, "We had a lousy relationship with our parents. It was one of those 'you just stay outside the door' things. It was really adversarial. And our schools were not welcoming. . . . We'd done some things around parent involvement and parent education, but it was really lip service."

DISTRICT REORGANIZATION

Upon her arrival, the new superintendent reportedly talked to as many people as she could in San Antonio to gain a deeper understanding of the schools' needs. Based on conversations with principals and teachers, the experiences of central office staff, and the knowledge she brought with her, the superintendent proceeded to draw up five district goals. The goals were developed to support and realize the mission statement she constructed soon after her arrival:

> to be an urban school district where all students are achieving above state and national standards. Where they exhibit personal growth and where they are of service to others.

The district aimed to:

- Increase student achievement;

- Foster collaboration and communication;

- Strengthen parent and community involvement;

- Build an infrastructure for professional development; and

- Provide appropriate school facilities to all students.

With this framework in place, the central office took the first of many steps to move toward its goals. To ensure that the district could effectively support its campuses, the superintendent critically examined its organization as well as the leadership in place at schools.

Instructional Leadership at the District Level

To facilitate the realization of the district's five new goals, the superintendent first set out to build an infrastructure to support instruction. She began by eliminating certain central office positions, creating new ones, and reallocating resources to better serve schools. Her vision was to create a balanced blend of site-based and central operations management. As one central office administrator stated:

> You know, we have to come to terms with what really makes sense to be consistent district wide and what really the schools should be able to decide.

Central office staff were hired or reassigned to provide schools with instructional leadership. At the district level, four people were hired to serve as Instructional Stewards, or area superintendents. The Instructional Stewards were required to report directly to the superintendent. Each was held accountable for his or her own Learning Community, a specified group of elementary, middle, and high schools. The primary responsibility of the Instructional Stewards was to support schools and provide instructional guidance. The Instructional Stewards were expected to provide support by assisting the analysis of school data such as TAAS results and supervising the development of campus improvement plans. They were to study the campus plans of every school in their respective Learning Communities to assess their viability as well as commitment to San Antonio district goals.

In the words of one Instructional Steward, "Curriculum, instruction, assessment is what we're all about." Another reported that Instructional Stewards were "responsible for supporting the principals, of evaluating them, of helping them to determine the priority needs within their schools and supporting them in accomplishing whatever it is they needed to accomplish."

Although the responsibilities of Instructional Stewards did not include dealing with school operations and maintenance, at times they found themselves engaged in such work. As one of the Stewards stated:

> We end up dealing with facilities because whatever is of a concern to the principal really becomes a concern for us.

In addition, each Instructional Steward was given other assignments. For example, each was required to sit on task forces (such as the Bilingual Task Force or the Race and Class Task Force), oversee the logistics of professional development, and/or supervise the implementation of particular NAS designs.

Instructional Leadership at the School Level

At the school level, the superintendent reinforced her instructional emphasis by assessing the principals in place and replacing those who tended to neglect instruction. Because the school board chose the principals prior to the superintendent's arrival, the principal appointments tended to be mired in politics. The superintendent tried to neutralize this by establishing screening committees at the school level that included representatives of different constituencies. The various groups made their recommendations, and the superintendent looked for people who could show her data, interpret the data, and plan a course of action based on collected information. In all, 40 new principals were hired, replacing many who left of their own volition.

The superintendent then created Instructional Guide positions to further facilitate communication and action around instructional practice. The Instructional Guides tended to be master teachers deemed highly competent, knowledgeable of curriculum and instruction, and able to readily communicate and anticipate the needs of others. They were hired to be their schools' instructional leaders, managing tasks that principals didn't have time for. The Instructional Guides also were expected to serve as liaisons between the district and their schools, communicating the central office's ideas to teachers and learning the various district initiatives to take back to their respective campuses. Furthermore, they were to facilitate the implementation of all new programs and provide teachers with in-house follow-up to professional development.

Instructional Guides received a great deal of credit for enabling the district office to push forward and implement ideas very rapidly. Quarterly meetings attended by Instructional Guides and central office staff served to further the budding lines of communication. During these meetings, the Guides reportedly discussed what was working at their schools, what upset teachers, what needed to be improved upon, and what additional support systems were necessary.

Collaboration and Communication

The superintendent's attempts to restructure and redefine leadership at both the district and school levels were all part of her plan to build the infrastructure necessary to support instruction and foster collaboration and communication within the district. Meetings were arranged between the central office and principals from particular Learning Communities. Moreover the same school-level principals regularly met together as well. The superintendent held teacher coffees once a month open to all who wished to communicate with her and with one another. Schools were encouraged to make time for their teachers to sit down together and discuss issues. The central office also created teacher networks to promote communication across school lines. Moreover, plans were made for schools to be connected via the World Wide Web.

Collaboration and communication were further facilitated through district- and school-level leadership committees, established in January of 1994, and referred to as the San Antonio Leadership Team (SALT) and Instructional Leadership Teams (ILTs), respectively. Like many other Texas school districts, the San Antonio school district, via ILTs, moved to give its schools the authority to decide how best to improve their respective educational records. The premise behind the district leadership team, or SALT, was to increase the representation of voices involved in making a variety of school-related decisions.[2]

Curriculum and Instruction

In an effort to raise test scores and ensure that all students learn particular skills and increase their knowledge base, the central office set out to develop an instructional framework to guide teachers. Originally, curriculum and instruction were the responsibility of Instructional Stewards. An Office of Curriculum and Instruction, overseen by the Associate Superintendent, was created in 1997 to help establish a coherent academic vision for the district. The central office wanted to make sure that comparable instruction, in line with state-developed academic standards, could be found occurring at the same grade levels across all district campuses. In the words of one central office administrator:

> The whole issue of the standards came about after our reflection that that's what we needed. We decided we'd go with Texas, essential elements and skills. But we also needed something as a district, because we were just all over the place.

Moreover, it was believed that district-endorsed mathematics and reading initiatives could help alleviate the difficulties stemming from the district's high rate of student mobility. Additionally, the Office of Curriculum and Instruction could work to ensure that all teachers (particularly those new to the field) know how to teach core subjects. In the words of one Instructional Steward:

> I think the primary reason [the Office of] Curriculum and Instruction was established was we're a district of teachers who have been

---

[2]According to the district's 1998–1999 Resource Guide for School Improvement, "District and campus level planning and decision-making committees were established to provide input and to assist in establishing and reviewing the district's and campus's educational plans, goals, performance objectives, and major classroom instructional programs. Both SALT and the ILTs serve exclusively in advisory capacities to the superintendent and principals, respectively, addressing such areas as curriculum, staffing, budgeting, school organization, and staff development." Each committee's members consist of a team of selected and appointed teachers, parents, community members, and business representatives. Additionally, paraprofessionals, classified staff members, and students sit on ILTs.

here 25–30 years or very young teachers with very little experience. So they come, especially in this state now, with the inability even to teach reading, because they don't know how. So by having [an Office of] Curriculum and Instruction focusing on that and teaching these teachers how to teach, because they really haven't in their college experience had that, maybe we can create a critical mass of teachers with experience who have good strategies that ultimately with principals and community could get the kinds of learning going on in schools that these kids need.

The Office of Curriculum and Instruction quickly decided to focus its efforts on research-based instructional initiatives targeting the two most basic subjects, mathematics and reading. In mathematics, the staff decided to continue endorsing the Everyday Mathematics program, which the central office had told all schools to adopt in the spring of 1996.[3] Prior to that spring, schools were asked to voluntarily implement the program.[4]

A research-based reading initiative, Balanced Literacy and Widening Parameters, was implemented during the 1996–1997 school year. The initiative served to provide teachers not only with training on literacy instruction (i.e., how to teach reading) but also with the materials necessary to enable students to succeed, such as books and appropriate workbooks. Instructional Guides were made responsible for ensuring that teachers understood the components of the literacy training and the strategies involved in teaching them.[5] During the

---

[3]Everyday Mathematics (EDM) is a K–12 curriculum developed by the University of Chicago School Mathematics Project. The curriculum assumes a spiraling approach to instruction where students are repeatedly exposed to key ideas, in greater depth each time. Key features of the Everyday Mathematics curriculum, described in teachers' manuals, include: problem solving about common-life situations; sharing ideas through discussions; daily routines; yearly projects; establishing links between past experiences and explanations of new concepts; cooperative learning through small group activities; practice through games; ongoing review throughout the year; informal assessment; and home/school partnership.

[4]After Everyday Mathematics had been in place for three years, teachers were given the opportunity to vote for or against it. In the spring of 1999, the curriculum was voted out in favor of a more traditional math program.

[5]Balanced Literacy was the name given the professional development program for pre-K through second grade teachers. Widening Parameters was the analogous training program for grade 3 through high school teachers. The following components were covered during elementary school teachers' professional development on literacy instruction: assessment procedures, reading instructions, literature studies,

1998–1999 school year, reading instruction became more standard-ized across the district. The central office asked teachers to engage in specific activities for particular amounts of time.

The district also moved to incorporate technology into instruction. It was not given the same attention by the Office of Curriculum and Instruction, however. Because the district office was eager to see its schools keep pace with technological advancements, it provided teacher training. Teachers were asked to teach their students certain computer skills and utilize computers as much as possible. The dis-trict developed a plan to provide Internet access to all schools. Class-rooms in every school were provided with several computers.

Professional Development

To fully support its instructional goals, the central office revamped its system of professional development. Instructional Guides were key to this change. As stated, they were seen as the primary source of on-site instructional support. In the words of one district adminis-trator:

> One of the things that we tried to do in supporting professional de-velopment was to make sure that we had some support right there on campus. So we really restructured Title I in saying, okay, we're going to put a person on every campus whose major job is to sup-port teachers through providing professional development, doing model teaching, finding the materials or instructional things that teachers need.

Like those in the Office of Curriculum and Instruction, staff involved in designing the district's professional development looked to re-search findings to define "good" professional development. Fur-thermore, they constructed professional development with their in-structional vision always in focus: "reforming schools to become

---

writing process instruction, grammar and mechanics, and language development. During training sessions, teachers learned about: modeled, shared, guided, paired, and independent reading; Individual Reading Inventories; The Reading Process; daily sustained silent reading; phonemic and structural analysis; grouping strategies; and how to address individual student needs. Included in the district's reading initiative in 1998–1999 was a McGraw-Hill Spelling Program for first through sixth grade students; teachers also received training for this program.

places where things are connected for students." They also made sure to develop a coherent series of workshops that included follow-up.

The district's renewed focus on instruction and emphasis on instructional leadership required that principals go through a professional development program customized to meet their individual needs. According to one district office staff member, Instructional Stewards put together a catalogue from which principals could pick and choose training sessions. Additionally, principals were required to attend training in areas where Instructional Stewards noticed weaknesses. At times, stewards strongly advised principals to receive professional development in certain areas, leaving the ultimate decision up to them. In the words of one Instructional Steward:

> we ask principals where they want to grow. We interact with all the departments and ask . . . where principal training is needed to address the needs of the department. If it's finance, . . . a department head may say, half of them turn in their budgets wrong. Then we know they need training in the finance area. Another way is when the Instructional Stewards work with principals [on a specific problem], for example conflict mediation. We may be going to campuses frequently because schools are faced with a number of grievances or they have a lot of parent complaints. Then a steward would say, well I need for my principal to go through this.

Similar opportunities were developed for teachers. Professional development was designed with a heavy emphasis on mathematics and reading. As stated, the curriculum and instruction staff felt it especially important to provide teachers with instructional strategies. Furthermore, they were determined to see the district's schools meet the state's standards of instruction. Technology was pushed in part for this reason. In fact, the district stipulated in newer teacher contracts that teachers become skilled in the use of technology within three years.

Parent and Community Involvement

The superintendent's administration attempted to address parent and community involvement issues as well. A Parent Community Partnership Network was formed with grant money attached to the

Rockefeller Initiative. By creating an office to support parents, the superintendent aimed to further enhance the infrastructure needed to foster high-quality instructional delivery.

NEW AMERICAN SCHOOLS IN SAN ANTONIO

While restructuring instructional leadership, rethinking the delivery and content of professional development, introducing instructional strategies to teachers, pushing state standards, and refocusing the district's attention on instruction and student achievement, San Antonio district administrators simultaneously reviewed national reform efforts and programs. One idea central office administrators seriously examined and eventually decided to implement was that forwarded by NAS, namely comprehensive school reform.

Initially, the superintendent introduced one NAS design, ELOB. This occurred soon after her arrival. It was a design she had overseen while serving as superintendent in Dubuque, Iowa. In fact, she had been influential in the development of the ELOB design early on in the NAS initiative.

Soon after the superintendent came to San Antonio and encouraged the district schools to implement the ELOB design, NAS invited San Antonio to become one of its jurisdiction sites. The superintendent committed the financial resources necessary to bring the NAS designs to the district.

The superintendent viewed designs as the needed catalyst to force schools to examine change from within. She did not want the piecemeal practice of reform to continue within the district's schools, where only certain classrooms or subject teachers engaged in new practices. Not only did she view the NAS designs as the outside galvanizing force for change, she also had hopes that the designs would help sustain the district's efforts to engage in comprehensive school reform. Others in the central office thought, too, that the NAS designs could "provide a wholeness and integration and stimulate teachers to think or rethink what they were doing." The designs also were seen as one way to help shift teachers' thinking as isolated agents of instruction to members of a community of learners. "When you've got a whole-school design, everybody plays, everybody's part of the planning process." In the words of one district staff member:

You've really got a nice framework to plan for all the professional development, and how we're going to deal with curriculum, and where parents fit in, and what kind of support system we need to have and what are the materials. It just really is such a help for any kind of school to really finally get a coherent plan, a framework, to get everybody moving in the same direction. You know, we got everybody working hard but not always moving in the same direction. I think all those designs are a wonderful aid to us.

THE INTRODUCTION OF NAS DESIGNS TO SCHOOLS

Convinced that the designs could play an important role in the district's efforts to bring about increased student achievement by compelling all staff in a school building to engage in comprehensive reform, the central office approached the schools via the Instructional Stewards. Initially, four designs were selected to be introduced to schools within the district: MRSH, ELOB, Co-NECT, and SFA/RW. Orientations in the form of site visits, design fairs, and design-centered conversations were offered to familiarize school staff and administrators with each design's philosophy and elements. Design literature was distributed as well. Schools were told that the district would provide the financial resources needed to implement their designs of choice. During the first round of district-wide design push, the schools were not forced to select a design. Teachers were told, however, that within three years, all of the district's schools would be expected to have one in place.

Before the district actually became a NAS jurisdiction, the central office required that only 60 percent of a school's staff be in support of the only design introduced at that time, ELOB. During the second phase of introduction, the office raised the support rate to 70 percent. Still the district found that those who opposed adoption were great enough in number to significantly impede design implementation. Thus, upon becoming a NAS jurisdiction and introducing schools to more designs at the end of the 1995–1996 school year, the district required that 80 percent of any school's staff be in favor of their selected design.

According to the accounts of teachers and other school staff, decisions to adopt particular designs, as well as the reasons for doing so, tended to vary by school. At some schools, the principals strongly encouraged their teachers to consider a particular design. At other schools, teachers were directed to choose what they thought would work best. Some schools felt more pressure than others to decide upon a design. A number of teachers expressed that they had been told that should they select a design right away, their school would be guaranteed the money needed for implementation. Many teachers said that they felt somewhat rushed to make a decision. After their designs of choice had been implemented and the teachers had had some time to reflect, many came to believe that they did not have sufficient information to make the decisions they had made. Some expressed that they were not aware how involved and labor-intensive design implementation would be. Others remarked that certain aspects of their schools' designs appealed to them more than others, leading them to make the decisions they made. In some cases, this worked out well. In others, teachers felt that their understanding of designs had been faulty from the start.

The adoption of SFA/RW differed significantly from the other designs. Given the district's focus on reading (as well as math), the reading component of Roots & Wings known as Success for All drew schools to this design. It's not clear whether all components of RW were even introduced. None of the SFA/RW schools we visited implemented more than the SFA program. Interviews with teachers suggested that they were not aware if plans were in the works to implement other components of the RW design.

THE DISTRICT'S ROLE IN SUPPORTING COMPREHENSIVE SCHOOL REFORM

Viewing NAS designs as the framework and glue to hold the multiple district initiatives together, the central office expected to monitor the progress of design implementation and support the schools in their efforts. It provided Instructional Guides, professional development, and financial resources. For schools that decided upon MRSH and Co-NECT, the district expended great effort to wire the schools quickly. According to one administrator, "We had always put dollars in to try to cable schools. But what we did was shift them to make sure that our priorities were always project Co-NECT and MRSH."

As time passed, it became clear to central staff members and design team representatives alike that greater communication was needed between them. The district took the initiative by arranging quarterly meetings to be attended by all design representatives, Instructional Stewards, and several central office staff members. These meetings began in the 1998–1999 academic year.

It was important to all involved to determine how best to align the designs with the district's plan for professional development and emphasis on state-developed academic standards. There had been confusion regarding this because in some cases the district initiatives unintentionally, but directly, conflicted with the principles of various designs. Moreover, when there was overlap between district and design ideas regarding instructional practice, the teachers often did not know which to follow. In the words of a central office administrator:

> I understand schools' frustration with NAS fitting into the district's plan of school improvement because it's hard. It is hard for them. And I'm not sure . . . it's one of my biggest stresses right now. How do I help them? I'm not sure yet.

It was important to the central office that schools not perceive the designs as "add-ons" to current district initiatives.

At these meetings with design representatives, the central office strived to better define its role in the design implementation process. Discussions revolved around design-generated benchmarks, student achievement, and curriculum, for example. With respect to benchmarks, the central office wished specifically to receive design team assessments regarding their respective views of implementation progress. However, representatives from all designs except SFA/RW (already an exception to the others, given the district's adoption of SFA only) were reluctant to provide such feedback for fear of jeopardizing their relationships with schools. Eventually, the design teams modified their positions to accommodate the district's request.

The district sought assessments of implementation progress not only to determine the fruits of its investment in NAS designs, but also to determine areas of weakness in schools' comprehensive reform efforts.

IMPACT OF INCREASING STATE ACCOUNTABILITY

Clearly, the operating environment into which NAS designs were introduced was in great flux. The district's efforts to construct an infrastructure for professional development and to foster collaboration and communication among district administrators, principals, teachers, school staff, and parents rattled the status quo, causing many in the schools to react tentatively as they adjusted to the stresses brought about by change.

The emphasis placed by the district on increasing student achievement and aligning curriculum with state-endorsed standards further escalated the pressure that teachers felt in their efforts to make sense of the district restructuring and to learn the information and practices new to them. Compounding this pressure was the increased emphasis on their students' TAAS performance. Given the low performance of the district's students on TAAS, and the new administration's focus on increased student achievement, the push to increase standardized test scores grew ever stronger each year.

Pressure was attached to testing success given the use of TAAS scores to determine school ratings. Each year, the Texas Education Agency (TEA) rates schools as "exemplary," "recognized," "academically acceptable," and "low performing" based on TAAS results, annual dropout rates (not included for elementary schools), and student attendance. These factors are not weighted. To receive a given rating, a school must meet all of the minimum requirements for that rating. For example, a school with a 100 percent TAAS pass rate would still receive a *Low* rating if the attendance rate were below 94 percent. The following table defines the different ratings.

Table 3.1

School Ratings

	Exemplary	Recognized	Acceptable	Low
Minimum pass rate (%)[a]	90+	75+	35+	< 35
Dropout rate (%)	≤ 1	≤ 3.5	≤ 6	> 6
Attendance rate (%)	≥ 94	≥ 94	≥ 94	< 94

[a]Minimum pass rate required not only of students overall, but of each student group on campus as well (African American, Hispanic, white, and economically disadvantaged) in each tested subject area: reading, writing, and mathematics.

The ratings of individual schools annually appeared in the local newspaper, pushing school staff and administrators to achieve student success in the name of pride. Moreover, "low performing" schools faced any of a number of sanctions listed in the Texas Education Code. They ranged from publicly notifying the board of trustees of a campus's deficiencies to appointing a board of managers comprised of district residents to exercise the powers and duties normally assumed by the district's board of trustees. In the worst cases, where schools had been found low performing for at least two years, campus closure was threatened.

The district obviously wanted to see its schools succeed and perform well on TAAS. Moreover, for purposes of determining its own accreditation status, the district desired success in its own right.

A financial incentive to demonstrate improvement or sustained success on TAAS was introduced by the state in 1995 under the leadership of the 74th legislature, whereupon the 75th Texas legislature appropriated $5 million for dispersal during the 1997–1998 and 1998–1999 school years. The money was used to fund the Texas Successful Schools Award System (TSSAS). Schools rated as "acceptable," "recognized," or "exemplary" were eligible to receive TSSAS awards ranging from $500 to $5,000 if they met specified criteria with respect to attendance, dropout rates, and passing rates of all students and each student group on the various sections of TAAS. An additional criterion that qualified schools for a TSSAS award was their rating in reading and math. Eligible schools had to "be ranked in the top quartile of their unique comparison group" in both reading and math.[14]

SUMMARY

The multitude of changes initiated by the district in a number of areas, namely school and district leadership, professional development, communication, and curriculum and instruction, propelled teachers and school administrators to critically examine organizational and instructional practices and to engage in steps needed to bring about envisioned change. Simultaneously, the district and

---

[14]See http://www.tea.state.tx.us.

schools felt increasing pressure to improve TAAS performance given renewed focus on instruction, students' low scores, impending state sanctions for poor performance, and desire for both decent campus accountability ratings and financial rewards for achievement.

This was the context in which NAS designs were introduced. Given the many reform initiatives in place, as well as the speed with which changes were occurring, the dynamic operating environment proved over time to be less supportive than expected. To illustrate some of these changes, the next chapter describes further the school context in which NAS designs were implemented. The findings are based on our analysis of our longitudinal teacher sample (40 teachers), observations, interviews, and district and school documents.

Chapter Four

IMPLEMENTATION OF NEW AMERICAN SCHOOLS WITHIN A SYSTEM OF HIGH-STAKES ACCOUNTABILITY

In the spring of 1998, a look inside San Antonio schools and classrooms implementing New American Schools designs would have led one to believe that the transition from design selection to implementation had been successful to date. In MRSH schools, for example, one saw standards posted ubiquitously on classroom walls and in hallways next to abundant displays of student work. In SFA/RW schools, posters of hand signals for classroom management purposes were taped to the hallway walls. Classrooms and bulletin boards alike were print-rich. All students engaged in 90 minutes of reading instruction at the same time every day and were expected to read for 20 minutes every night. In ELOB schools, posters of the design's principles were found in classrooms and on hallway walls; drafts and redrafts of student work were openly displayed. Teachers developed expeditions into which they incorporated project work. In Co-NECT schools, students utilized computers to conduct research and frequently worked on interdisciplinary projects in small groups.

The NAS proposal was introduced to San Antonio schools by the district with hopes that the marketed "break the mold" designs would provoke teachers and administrators to engage enthusiastically in comprehensive school reform. The thought was that an external model provider would be more successful at pushing and sustaining change than the central office could ever be alone. The district had every intention of fully supporting its NAS schools in all ways. Not only did it plan to pay for the services of design teams in its schools, it aimed to provide instructional support via the Instructional Stewards and Guides. Moreover, the district moved toward granting its schools the autonomy to make school-specific instructional decisions.

Given this, in 1996, when NAS designs were first introduced, one might have expected that in time, design schools would look, feel, and in some ways function differently from one another as well as from schools that had elected not to take on comprehensive school reform models.

However, a closer examination of both whole-school and individual classroom activities tended to reveal a more complicated story. In this chapter, we present our findings from the perspective of schools, focusing on the factors in NAS schools that were important for design implementation. With information from our surveys (i.e., the longitudinal sample of 40 teachers) and fieldwork, we focus here on the challenging educational environments that these schools faced, the high-stakes accountability system in which they operated, the process for adopting NAS designs, support for implementation including training and professional development, principal leadership, and teacher collaboration and support of the NAS designs.

NAS DESIGNS PROVIDED ASSISTANCE TO CHALLENGING SCHOOLS

NAS design teams assisted lower-performing schools in San Antonio, facing many challenges—as was the case in other jurisdictions (see Berends, 1999; Berends and Kirby et al., 2001).

In Texas, the relative performance of individual schools is determined each spring by the TEA. Ratings are issued based on a combination of factors that include average performance on the TAAS, attendance, and dropout rates. Schools are rated "low performing," "acceptable," "recognized," or "exemplary." We calculated average annual ratings for NAS and non-NAS schools from the 1995 through 1999 school years as shown in Figure 4.1; for this figure, we examined all schools that were NAS by the 1998–1999 school year and tracked their ratings back in time. In 1995, test scores throughout the district placed all schools below the acceptable rating (averages for NAS and non-NAS schools were 1.96 and 1.97, respectively).

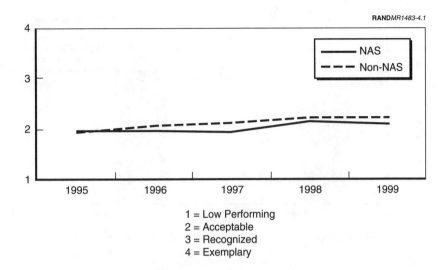

Figure 4.1—Average Texas Education Agency Ratings for Schools in
San Antonio, 1995–1999[1]

The state officially assigned the district a "warning" status that year, putting it on notice to improve.   After 1995, average ratings improved at a higher rate for non-NAS schools than for NAS schools. By 1999, the rating for NAS schools was 2.10, while the average rating of non-NAS schools was 2.24.

The premise that schools adopting NAS designs tended to be lower performing than the non-NAS schools was borne out by differences in teachers' perceptions of their students. In both the 1998 and the 1999 surveys, teachers were asked to rate the average academic ability of students in their classes compared with "the national average." In 1999, 77 percent of the NAS teachers reported that the academic ability of their students was below the national norm compared with 36 percent of non-NAS teachers (see Figure 4.2). Although this perception of both NAS and non-NAS teachers increased from the year

_____

[1]The NAS designation includes any elementary schools that had adopted NAS models by the 1998–1999 school year. The non-NAS schools are the other elementary schools in the district.

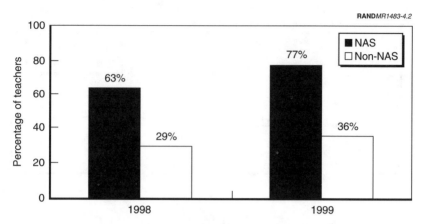

NOTE: Percentages are based on a total sample size of 40 teachers—26 NAS and 14 Non-NAS.

**Figure 4.2—Percentage of Teachers Who Reported That the Academic
Ability Level of Their Students Was Below the National Norm
in NAS and Non-NAS Schools, Spring 1998 and 1999**

before, the more important point to note is that a significantly greater percentage of NAS teachers than non-NAS ones reported their students' academic ability as being below the national norm.

Teachers also reported on a variety of factors that moderately or greatly hindered their students' academic success, including the students' lack of basic skills, motivation, or discipline; inadequate preparation in subject areas; student mobility; inadequate support from parents; student advancement to next grade without meeting promotion requirements; and poor student attendance (see Table 4.1). In each category and in each year, substantially higher percentages of teachers in the NAS schools reported that specific factors hindered student achievement, indicating the types of educational challenges they faced in their schools and classrooms.

Although average TAAS test scores and TEA ratings increased for both NAS and non-NAS schools between 1998 and 1999, teachers' perceptions of their students' academic abilities tended to become more negative. In general, schools that chose to adopt NAS designs,

Table 4.1

Percentage of Teachers Who Reported That the Following Factors Moderately or Greatly Hindered Student Academic Success

	1998		1999	
	NAS	Non-NAS	NAS	Non-NAS
Lack of basic skills	85%	71%	100%	79%
Inadequate prior student preparation in the subject areas	96%	71%	92%	71%
Lack of student motivation	81%	57%	81%	57%
Student advancement to next grade without meeting promotion requirements	85%	64%	73%	64%
Lack of student discipline	58%	36%	62%	43%
High student mobility in and out of the school	85%	43%	73%	57%
Inadequate support from parents for students	73%	43%	77%	57%
Poor student attendance	58%	36%	42%	29%

NOTE: Percentages are based on teacher reports in a total sample size of 40 teachers—26 NAS and 14 Non-NAS.

or were encouraged by the district to do so, tended to be lower performing relative to other schools in the district.

PRESSURES TO IMPROVE STATE TEST SCORES

The press to increase student achievement and improve test scores in San Antonio schools was clearly evident during the time of our study. To this end, the district, under the superintendent's leadership, actively engaged itself in the process of reorganizing in accord with the U.S. Department of Education's criteria defining comprehensive school reform.[2] District staff were aware of these federal cri-

---

[2]Critical components of schoolwide designs under the federal CSRD program include curriculum and instruction, content and performance standards, assessments, pro-

teria during the 1998-1999 school year and began to examine their district educational reform initiatives according to them. Toward that end, the district established an Office of Curriculum and Instruction responsible for developing a sequential, standards-aligned curriculum across grade levels in all schools throughout the district. The core subjects—namely mathematics and reading and an emphasis on standards—were given primary attention at first because of

---

fessional development, school organization and governance issues, and parent involvement. According to the program, "a comprehensive school reform program is one that integrates, in a coherent manner, all nine of the following components":

1. Employs innovative strategies and proven methods for student learning, teaching, and school management that are based on reliable research and effective practices, and have been replicated successfully in schools with diverse characteristics;

2. Has a comprehensive design for effective school functioning, including instruction, assessment, classroom management, professional development, parent involvement, and school management, that aligns the school's curriculum, technology, professional development into a schoolwide reform plan designed to enable all students to meet challenging state content and performance standards and addresses needs identified through a school needs assessment;

3. Provides high-quality and continuous teacher and staff professional development and training;

4. Has measurable goals for student performance tied to the state's challenging content and performance standards, as those standards are implemented, and benchmarks for meeting those goals;

5. Is supported by school faculty, administrators and staff;

6. Provides for the meaningful involvement of parents and the local community in planning and implementing school improvement activities;

7. Utilizes high-quality external technical support and assistance from a comprehensive school reform entity (which may be a university) with experience or expertise in schoolwide reform and improvement;

8. Includes a plan for the evaluation of the implementation of school reforms and the student results achieved; and

9. Identifies how other resources (federal, state, local, and private) available to the school will be utilized to coordinate services to support and sustain the school reform.

Schools and districts have considerable latitude in developing strategies to achieve the program's goals, provided these strategies encompass the nine defined components listed above. The legislation provides a list of school reform models as *examples*. The guidance in the legislation encourages schools to consider other models (or their combination) that have evidence of effectiveness. Indeed, schools can create their own models of schoolwide reform by using a combination of approaches to curriculum instruction, assessment, and organization reform. The aim is to implement *effective, schoolwide* improvement strategies (see http://www.ed.gov/offices/OESE/compreform).

the low achievement of the district's students. According to a top district administrator, the central office was attempting to bring "an intense instructional focus to the district, supported by quality programs and professional development—intense . . . professional development, not shoot from the hip, one-shot kind of deals."

Additionally, the district partnered with New American Schools to help tighten its focus and to encourage school improvement. Suddenly, schools were not only exposed to many ideas, but required to implement them at once, naturally resulting in some confusion and resistance on the part of school staff.

The emphasis on increased student achievement not only called for greater student learning, it heightened the district's focus on improved TAAS performance as well. Tied to the Texas system of school accountability, TAAS scores provided concrete measures of achievement readily reported to and understood by administrators and teachers alike. The act of addressing targeted skills enabled educators to work toward specific academic goals during a time of great change in the district. Based on our classroom observations and conversations with teachers, it appeared that successful TAAS performance became not only the goal easiest to visualize but in fact *the* goal to attain. Schools paid a price for this, however. According to teachers, the focus on TAAS tended to mute creativity and channel all activities toward preparation as the test approached. About half the teachers we talked with reported incorporating test-taking strategies and TAAS vocabulary into their lessons from day one of the school year.

> We are very TAAS focused at the beginning of the year. A lot of us would think in that direction from the beginning when you start learning how to highlight in the book and pick out what is important. There are a lot of strategies that we teach that start off from the very beginning in all the lessons. (SFA/RW)

> I think TAAS takes up pretty much the day, and I think as teachers we get bogged down with those worksheets and don't come up with other creative ways to implement the objectives that they test on in TAAS. So I think we're very worksheet oriented because I think when the children do get that test booklet, it won't be in the form of

> a game, it won't be in the form of a project. But it would be in pa-
> per, pencil test. (ELOB)

> When you plan and divide kids up, you're always getting ready, get-
> ting prepared for TAAS, getting instructed in TAAS, getting the kids
> ready for it. Your instructional time, you know, you're heavy into
> the reading. (Co-NECT)

In addition, lack of time during the school day—a chronic issue—
became even more problematic in light of teachers' needs to balance
TAAS preparation with other instruction. Many teachers reportedly
coped with the multiple demands on their time by putting aside
other activities to focus almost exclusively on TAAS as the test dates
grew closer.

> Come January, MRSH is over here, you know, on the side. . . . From
> January through the end of February, which is when we have our
> writing TAAS, we write compositions . . . we write all day, every day
> in the month of February. So then MRSH is out the window. . . .
> Maybe once a week we could do that, but you can't teach a unit
> once a week. And so it just doesn't happen. Okay, as soon as that's
> over [TAAS writing], like March 1st, then we're cramming for the
> TAAS-formatted math and reading. . . . And we do that for two
> months solid.

> Honestly, [TAAS] plays a very, very, very big role in how we structure
> time. . . . Starting in January, that's when it's pretty much drop ev-
> erything but the reading program, drop everything except SFA and
> TAAS.

During the 1998–1999 school year, schools administered as many as
four district-directed TAAS simulations, after which teachers were
required to analyze the results and pinpoint their students' weaknesses.

> [you] have assessments schoolwide that you have to do and figure
> out the percentage of students passing and write out a pass plan on
> how you can get those students who did not pass up to passing
> mode. You have to turn it in, a sheet with every student's name as
> to what objectives they have passed and what objectives they've
> failed.

> We give a TAAS simulation and if your class is extremely weak in a certain area, it is your [the teacher's] responsibility to boost that one target area.

In many classrooms, bar graphs were posted, revealing individual students' scores on each TAAS subtest. Interestingly, we heard from teachers of two low-performing schools that they were "encouraged" by the district to suspend all activity that did not directly stress TAAS skills. For one school, this meant neglecting its NAS design altogether in favor of engaging in basic skills instruction all year long. At the other school, the poor performance of their students on a TAAS simulation resulted in teachers being asked to suspend all design activity after spring break to prepare intensively for the upcoming test.

At several schools Instructional Guides remarked that 1998–1999 was the first year teachers were explicitly asked to "teach to TAAS." The administration disliked having to make such a request, but felt that their schools had no substantial say in the matter. Schools feared being placed on lists that threatened their existence. Moreover, a district policy enacted at the start of the 1998–1999 school year based teachers' evaluations in part on their students' TAAS scores. In the words of an Instructional Guide:

> Our TAAS scores are probably not where they should be. Therefore some other people influenced us a bit to do different things versus a Co-NECT model. So we haven't been able to focus on it as should be.... We really haven't been focusing on the Co-NECT model as we should at all.... We have always felt very strongly about . . . teaching. I mean really get in there and teach reading and teach math and . . . not spend a lot of time on how to take a test and this kind of thing. And we've been forced to turn around and do much more of that.

According to one teacher: "[The district] has just about threatened to disown schools who were doing ELOB because we weren't concentrating on TAAS. And TAAS is the be-all, end-all.... But we're seeing scores that are not acceptable."

Whether or not schools were directly told to focus on TAAS preparation, teachers at all schools in our sample reported feeling pressure to "teach to TAAS" given the high-stakes nature of the test.

To help students perform better on TAAS, teachers spent time not only on reviewing the skills that would be tested, but also on the art of test-taking. This included teaching test-taking strategies and exposing students to test vocabulary, wording, and format.

> And then we practice with bubbles, transferring back and forth. And they've got to have a, b, c, d, e, and f. . . . And they really have to practice and practice and practice with that. And I don't know why it is so hard. . . . I would like to know why it is so difficult for them to make the transfer. (MRSH)

> It's how to read and understand what it's asking because if you understand what the TAAS is looking for, you can figure out how to answer it. . . . As we teach skills we teach strategies with it and figure out exactly which strategy is appropriate for this question. (SFA/RW)

> we try to format anything we do the way [TAAS] is given. (SFA/RW)

> the kids are not . . . familiar enough with the format of the question or the vocabulary. (Co-NECT)

It is within this context of high-stakes accountability, challenged schools, and high expectations for school improvement that the NAS designs were introduced to and implemented in schools.

ADOPTION OF DESIGNS

Upon talking with teachers, principals, and district staff, it became clear that the process by which teachers learned about NAS designs varied somewhat from campus to campus. Teachers at some schools reported being exposed to all the designs supported by the district— Co-NECT, ELOB, MRSH, and SFA/RW. Others heard about only a select few. A number of schools in our sample sent a select group of teachers to design presentations. These teachers then came back to their schools to share what they learned with their colleagues so that all could vote on their design of choice. Some schools had teachers visit actual design schools and report back to their colleagues. In some cases, teachers listened to the presentations of design representatives at their own schools. In the MRSH schools, the principals introduced the design to their teachers after each visited a demonstration site. Though teachers at these schools were told about at least one other design, MRSH seemed to be the one favored as it was introduced.

Regardless of the number of designs to which each school was introduced, all teachers across our sample were given the opportunity to vote. At many of the schools exposed to multiple designs, teachers first discussed the suitability of each to their respective campuses, then approved the design most favored through a vote. In some cases, all presented designs were listed as choices to be voted on. Early on, in accordance with district policy, at least 60 percent of all teachers and school staff had to vote in favor of a given design for it to be implemented.

Across our sample of NAS schools, teachers reported feeling pressure to choose a design. Given that in time all district schools were expected to take on a design, teachers never had the choice to reject design adoption altogether. Some non-NAS principals, however, reported during interviews they were able to resist initial adoption of a design because their schools were performing better than others. They told us that their colleagues in lower-performing schools had less of a choice in the matter.

Interviewer: Did the school feel pressure to adopt a design?

Teacher: Yes. Yes, we did. We were pretty much told either pick it now or we'll pick it for you later. (Co-NECT)

Teacher: Yes, definitely. We were pressured. We were pressured to adopt a design. (ELOB)

Teacher: Most definitely. Yes. (MRSH)

Teacher: Right. We had to [choose a design]. (SFA/RW)

Not only was there pressure to take on a design, several teachers stated that they were given little time to learn about and decide upon a comprehensive reform model. According to one of our MRSH teachers: "I remember that it was a rush, rush thing . . . and I know that at the time we voted on it, we had no idea what it was. . . . All we were told was the teacher would have a lot of input." In the words of the Instructional Guide at one of the SFA/RW schools, "I think there could have been more time exploring the designs, but on the other hand you can over-examine maybe some things." The Instructional Guide at one of our ELOB schools stated, "Truthfully, I felt that we could have and should have looked at other designs. But because of the time constraints, we had to immediately decide, and we did not get an opportunity to look at as many designs as there are out there."

Teachers reported choosing designs that seemed to match their schools' visions and instructional approaches. For many this meant going with the design that required the least change. Teachers at one Co-NECT school, for example, stated that this design over the others suited them best given that they already had reworked their curriculum and were unwilling to rewrite it:

> As a staff what we were looking for was something that would fit what we already have. . . . We weren't willing to chuck all the work that we had already done. . . . Co-NECT allowed us to keep the curriculum that we had and perhaps enhance it with technology.

The community engagement aspect of Co-NECT appealed to teachers as well. At our other Co-NECT school, teachers already employed project-based learning and technology to some extent, making this design more appealing. In the words of one teacher:

> planning projects we've always done. We've always worked on a thematic basis, even before Co-NECT was here and that was one reason why we chose it because we felt that it would be easier for us to implement.

At one of the SFA/RW schools, teachers stated that having to write thematic-based units turned them off to their other choices. In the case of our ELOB schools, the design principles and project-based approach to instruction appealed to teachers and school staff.

Thus, while teachers were attracted to certain aspects of NAS designs and were given the opportunity to vote to adopt a particular design, the time constraints to make a decision inhibited a greater understanding of what teachers could accomplish with a NAS design in place.

As for the two schools in our sample that had decided not to adopt a design early on, the teachers at both found that they had enough to do just implementing the district-required initiatives. The teachers we spoke with reported that their schools were in the process of investigating the various NAS designs and considering which one would work best in their respective buildings. Unlike the teachers at NAS schools, the teachers at the non-NAS schools we visited reported not feeling pressure to adopt a design right away.

DISTRICT ASSISTANCE FOR DESIGN IMPLEMENTATION

All schools, whether NAS or non-NAS, received increased support for teachers in the form of Instructional Guides. The Guides assumed responsibility for handling all curricular issues on campus and for keeping abreast of the latest instructional strategies and techniques. When needed, they assisted teachers in classrooms by modeling skills, for example. Instructional Guides also helped to identify and locate resources. Not only did they tutor and test students, they provided training to school staff as well. Furthermore, they worked closely with their respective principals, serving to facilitate communication between teachers and administrators. Given their many roles, Instructional Guides tended not to spend as much time in classrooms as they would have liked. Many reported that a good chunk of their time was spent away at training sessions. Instructional Guides at NAS schools attended both district in-services and design training.

When asked whether the district supported their schools' design implementation efforts, most teachers indicated that it did so passively. The central office allowed schools to choose from a selection of designs, for example. Additionally, it did not dictate how to proceed with design implementation. Most important, the district provided the funds to enable comprehensive school reform. Clear to teachers, however, was that the central office's emphasis was on test results. Thus, teachers in design schools were required to implement the district's mathematics and reading initiatives in addition to their reform models of choice. In this way, support from the central office for design implementation was conditional. According to one teacher:

> It's left up to the campus and the grade levels on how . . . to integrate all of this information. So I don't want to say that the district

doesn't support the design. They do, but they support just as much the things that the district is implementing onto the campuses as well.

PROFESSIONAL DEVELOPMENT

Professional development is a crucial element for school improvement (Bodilly, 2001; Garet et al., 1999). One of the challenges facing NAS schools has been that districts, not schools, control the resources for professional development. Districts also differ in the amount of funding they have to focus on specific professional development efforts for NAS design implementation. Moreover, some designs stress the importance of specific design team training for implementing the designs (e.g., MRSH and SFA/RW). Others (e.g., Co-NECT and ELOB) emphasize the importance of long-term development of teachers' capabilities and professionalization, which in turn should contribute to ongoing school improvement.   Whatever the approach, the availability of resources for design team training, district training, and overall professional development efforts for design implementation remains a challenge within districts that have competing goals, objectives, and incentives for teacher professional development.

Design Team Assistance

Besides the district and the Instructional Guides, design teams provide another important source of support for implementation. Design teams assist implementation by providing schools and teachers support such as training, professional development, and materials (Bodilly, 1998; Glennan, 1998). Each design team aims to provide schools and teachers with resources to assist in implementation, especially in terms of communication between design team members and school staff, and design-related professional development. Teachers' responses to our surveys provided a broad picture of how all design schools were progressing in implementation, and changes that occurred from one year to the next. For instance, in 1998 a relatively high proportion of teachers in the NAS schools (58 percent) agreed that each of their respective design teams had clearly communicated "its program to school staff so that it could be well-implemented." This type of communication improved in 1999 (88 percent of teachers agreed with this item).

Training by Design Teams

As for the actual design training, however, there was little regular, consistent assistance provided, according to teacher interviews across design schools. Over time, there was even less contact between teachers and their respective design representatives.

In large part, this had to do with the fact that these representatives serviced numerous schools, making it difficult for them to be attentive to any one. It also appears that from the start, strong relationships rarely were established, making it unlikely that teachers would rely on their respective design representatives for external technical support and assistance. In some schools, design representatives turned over, disrupting what rapport had been established. Several teachers in our sample saw their design representatives so infrequently that they didn't even know their names. The SFA/RW schools should have received the most regular design assistance given that each had one facilitator on campus to meet its needs. Additionally, the program included a series of implementation visits conducted by SFA consultants. At one of our SFA/RW schools, however, the Instructional Guide took on the SFA facilitator role as well, making it very difficult for her to efficiently address issues having to do with the design team's reading program.

Few design representatives entered classrooms on a regular basis. Teachers reported that visitors to classrooms tended to be district staff. The teachers were given little, if any, outside "expert" support that enabled them to objectively assess their progress and growth as design teachers. Teachers reported that when in need of help, they tended to turn to their colleagues or Instructional Guides first. Across design schools, teachers didn't have enough interaction with their respective design representatives to feel their absence.

In addition, teachers reported on our surveys that their participation in design-related professional development meetings/conferences declined from one year to the next. In 1998, 62 percent of teachers reported participating in these types of activities more than twice during the past 12 months; 50 percent of teachers reported doing so in 1999. The percentage of teachers who reported attending workshops or courses related to the NAS design also decreased from 50 percent in 1998 to 39 percent in 1999.

In part, these decreases may be due to design teams emphasizing teacher training more during the initial stages of implementation. However, the decline may also be a signal that the level of implementation itself was declining in these schools because the district was shifting its focus away from NAS efforts.

Consistent with the survey results, our interviews and observations revealed that teachers at ELOB, Co-NECT, and MRSH design schools saw their respective design representatives with little regularity—an impediment to design implementation. Regardless of their schools' adopted designs, teachers reported the need for more concrete, hands-on training that would enable them to better understand design processes.

A teacher at a Co-NECT school said that she would have found it helpful if at design training, participants were given concrete ways to involve the community in their school affairs, actual samples of Co-NECT products, and/or demonstrations of effective instructional strategies endorsed by Co-NECT, for example.

Teachers at MRSH schools expressed the need for workshops that actually demonstrated how to write units deemed high quality by MRSH standards and by the district/state standards. They felt that they had some sense as to what to incorporate; however, they didn't always know how to judge the quality of their work. Moreover, teachers expressed the need for workshops that actually taught Core Knowledge, a critical curricular component of MRSH. Not all teachers knew much about Islam and the Holy Wars, China, or the Middle Ages, for example.

Teachers at one SFA/RW school remarked that they would have found it helpful to periodically have SFA/RW representatives sit in their classrooms and provide feedback afterward. This way, any uncertainties they had about the program and its implementation could be immediately and effectively addressed.

Teachers at ELOB schools stated that they would have liked to see what defines a high-quality culminating project. They desired more assistance with respect to curriculum writing as well.

District Training and Professional Development

In addition to training by design teams, teachers at NAS schools also received the district's professional development, as did their colleagues from non-NAS schools. Much of the in-service professional development revolved around the district's reading and math initiatives. Teachers at SFA/RW schools attended reading in-services provided by the design rather than the district. Additional workshops for training in language arts instruction were offered during the 1998–1999 school year. Teachers attended technology training and workshops concerning state standards and curriculum alignment as well. Relatively speaking, few social studies or science workshops were provided.

Because NAS teachers were obligated to attend as many of these various in-services as their colleagues in non-NAS schools, the amount of training activities served only to heighten frustrations. All of the designs but SFA/RW required teachers to develop units and write curriculum. While encouraging schools to implement NAS designs, the district simultaneously constrained their ability to do so by telling teachers what to teach and how.

The district and design teams did not tend to coordinate their efforts with respect to professional development, so teachers were left on their own to merge the information they received from each. This was not easily done without modifying the essence of each design. Not only did this effort burden teachers' workload, it also led to confusion as to what to prioritize.

On our surveys, we asked several questions that addressed teacher participation in professional development activities not specifically related to the NAS designs. In general, compared with NAS teachers, a higher proportion of non-NAS teachers reported participation in a wide variety of professional development activities covering topics such as alternative student assessments, content standards, single-subject teaching areas, teaching techniques, classroom management, and educational technology. Respondents from the NAS schools indicated greater levels of participation in fewer activities: student portfolio development, assessment, and site-based management.

One survey item asked teachers the extent to which students' academic success was hindered by a lack of coherent, sustained professional development. As indicated in Figure 4.3, 31 percent of the NAS teachers reported that a lack of coherent professional development was a moderate or great problem in hindering students' academic success; this declined somewhat to 27 percent in 1999. Non-NAS teachers reported similarly on this measure in both 1998 and 1999.

Several survey items asked teachers about the quality of the professional development they received in the past year. Teachers indicated the extent to which they agreed or disagreed (4-point scale) that overall, "the professional development activities sponsored by the NAS design team, your school or the district," during the past 12 months had:

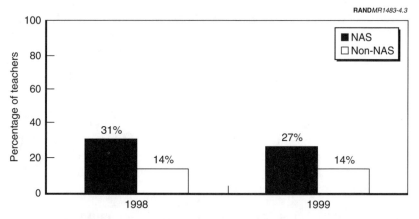

NOTE: Percentages are based on a total sample size of 40 teachers—26 NAS and 14 Non-NAS.

Figure 4.3—Percentage of Teachers Who Reported That a Lack of Coherent, Sustained Professional Development Hindered Students' Academic Success Moderately or Greatly in NAS and Non-NAS Schools, Spring 1998 and 1999

- Been sustained and coherently focused, rather than short-lived and unrelated;

- Included enough time to think carefully about, try, and evaluate new ideas;

- Been closely connected to the design team's activities in their school (NAS respondents only);

- Included opportunities to work productively with colleagues in their school;

- Deepened their understanding of the subject matter they teach;

- Led them to make changes in their teaching;

- Helped their school's staff work together better;

- Changed the way teachers talk about students in their school;

- Deepened their understanding of how students learn the subject matter they teach; and

- Altered approaches to teaching in their school.

We combined these items into a composite measuring the overall quality of professional development.[3]

Overall, less than 40 percent of all surveyed teachers reported that they agreed or strongly agreed that the professional development they received was of high quality (see Figure 4.4). In 1998, 38 percent of the NAS teachers reported that they agreed or strongly agreed across the items in the professional development composite compared with 27 percent of non-NAS teachers. In 1999, NAS teacher reports declined slightly (36 percent), while the non-NAS teacher reports increased slightly (29 percent).

PRINCIPAL LEADERSHIP

When considering implementation of NAS designs, an important school resource to note is the leadership of the principal. Other

---

[3]The alpha reliability of this quality of professional development composite was 0.92 for 1998 and 0.94 for 1999. The range of correlations for the individual items was 0.34 to 0.38 in 1998 and 0.45 to 0.50 in 1999.

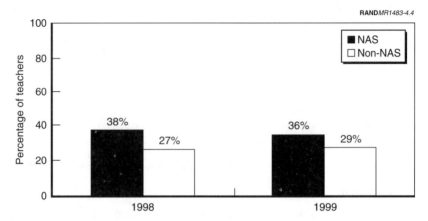

RAND*MR1483-4.4*

NOTE: Percentages are based on a total sample size of 40 teachers—26 NAS and 14 Non-NAS.

**Figure 4.4—Percentage of Teachers Who Agreed or Strongly Agreed with
High-Quality Professional Development Composite Items
in NAS and Non-NAS Schools, Spring 1998 and 1999**

studies have shown the importance of leadership in establishing effective school improvement efforts (Edmonds, 1979; Brookover et al., 1979; Purkey and Smith, 1983; Berends and Kirby et al., 2001). Based on our surveys, we found differences between NAS and non-NAS teachers' perceptions of principal leadership in their schools. For the principal leadership composite, teachers were asked the extent to which they agreed or disagreed (4-point scale) with the following statements:[4]

- The principal lets staff members know what is expected of them;

- The school administration's behavior toward the staff is supportive and encouraging;

- The principal does a poor job of getting resources for this school (reverse-scored);

---

[4]The alpha reliability for the principal leadership composite was 0.90 for 1998 and 0.84 for 1999. The range of correlations for the individual items was 0.38 to 0.47 in 1998 and 0.26 to 0.30 in 1999. More positive scores on this composite reflect more positive perceptions of teachers about principal leadership in their school.

- My principal enforces school rules for student conduct and backs me up when I need it;

- The principal talks with me frequently about my instructional practices;

- In this school, staff members are recognized for a job well done; and

- The principal has confidence in the expertise of the teachers.

Less than 40 percent of both the NAS and non-NAS teachers in both years agreed or strongly agreed that their principals were strong leaders according to these items (Figure 4.5). The generally low ratings on the principal leadership composite might be a reflection of the high level of curricular and programmatic change in the district, coupled with the pressure to improve student performance on the TAAS.

In both years, however, teachers in NAS schools reported higher scores on this principal leadership composite than teachers in non-

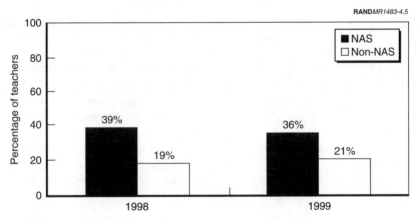

NOTE: Percentages are based on a total sample size of 40 teachers—26 NAS and 14 Non-NAS.

Figure 4.5—Percentage of Teachers Who Reported That They Agreed or Strongly Agreed with Principal Leadership Composite Items in NAS and Non-NAS Schools, Spring 1998 and 1999

NAS schools by 20 percentage points in 1998 and 15 percentage points in 1999. Previous studies have emphasized the importance of strong leadership in design implementation (Berends and Kirby et al., 2001; Kirby et al., 2001). However, in San Antonio, because each school had an Instructional Guide who took on some of the functions of instructional leader, perhaps teachers' reports across NAS and non-NAS schools reflect this delegation of tasks. The more positive perceptions of principal leadership in the NAS schools may reflect that these principals played an important role in facilitating the choice and adoptions of NAS designs in their schools.

TEACHER COLLABORATION

In addition to principal leadership, the implementation process for NAS designs hinges on teachers working together (Bodilly, 2001). The extent to which teachers coordinate their efforts, learn from each other, and work together to develop and/or teach the curriculum is critical for whole-school change (Louis and Marks, 1998; Louis et al., 1996; Newmann & Associates, 1996).

Because schools adopting NAS designs were expected to engage in teamwork, resulting in increased levels of cooperation among school staff, we measured teacher collaboration with a composite, combining several survey items. This composite was constructed from items that included a variety of response formats in which teachers were asked the extent to which the program elements described their schools (6-point scale ranging from does not describe my school to clearly describes my school), the extent to which items had changed in the past three years (5-point scale ranging from greatly improved to greatly worsened), and the extent to which they agreed or disagreed with statements (4-point scale ranging from strongly disagree to strongly agree). The following statements comprise the standardized teacher collaboration composite:[5]

---

[5]The alpha reliability for the teacher collaboration composite was 0.84 for 1998 and 0.85 for 1999. The range of correlations for the individual items was 0.39 to 0.53 in 1998 and 0.42 to 0.49 in 1999. Some items were reverse-scored so that a positive value on this composite reflected greater teacher collaboration. This unweighted composite was constructed by calculating standardized values (mean 0, variance 1) for each individual item within each year. These values were added together for each observation and then divided by the number of items used.

- Teachers are continual learners and team members through professional development, common planning, and collaboration;

- Teachers' learning from one another (worsened or improved);

- Most of my colleagues share my beliefs and values about what the central mission of the school should be;

- There is a great deal of cooperative effort among the staff members;

- Teachers respect other teachers who take the lead in school improvement efforts; and

- Teachers at this school respect those colleagues who are experts at their craft.

Overall, there was not much difference in the degree of teacher collaboration among teachers in NAS schools compared with those in non-NAS schools. Since the items in the teacher collaboration composite were not based on a common response metric, we report whether teacher responses for this composite were positive or negative on the standardized scale combining the different survey items. In both 1998 and 1999, 54 percent of NAS teachers scored positively on this composite. Exactly 50 percent of the non-NAS teachers' scores were positive in 1998. This rose to 57 percent in 1999.

Our interviews revealed that teachers generally praised the designs for nurturing collaboration among school staff. The designs themselves were unable to dissolve the teacher factions that existed at several schools, but they did bring about more teacher interaction and sharing of ideas according to our interviews with teachers. Additionally, the implementation of designs enabled teachers to be more aware of what their colleagues at other grade levels were responsible for teaching. Consequently, there was less overlap of subject material from one grade level to the next. A greater sense of unity developed among teachers as well with respect to curriculum, instructional strategies, and educational mission.

I find that that's one thing it's done is that we get together a whole lot more. Before you were pretty much in your room and you accomplished it and they'd come out and say here's your thing, and you know, you did it. But you didn't know what the others had done. You know, but now we're always . . . meeting and discussing and sharing papers. . . . So that to me has helped a lot because you don't feel like you're out there all alone. (Co-NECT)

I think on a grade level maybe, it gives us time to work together. Something to work for. (ELOB)

[The design is] getting the teachers better acquainted and mixed together so that we don't have factions in the building, like we used to. . . . And that [the MRSH design] has been kind of a common ground that we've all met on and that's helped. (MRSH)

[The design] is promoting more getting together within the grade level, and it opens up all of the lines of communication there, but I think grade level by grade level it changes. . . . (MRSH)

It is difficult to know, however, whether the designs themselves were solely responsible for such changes. Soon after her arrival, the superintendent aimed to build collaboration and communication not only between the district office and schools, but also within schools themselves. She encouraged every school to practice state-mandated site-based management, pushing for the institutionalization of campus-based advisory committees, referred to as Instructional Leadership Teams.[6] In essence, the teams, comprised of teachers, parents, community members, business representatives, paraprofessionals, classified staff members, and students, were responsible for oversee-

_____

[6]The implementation of site-based management was mandated for all Texas school districts in 1992. According to the TEA, campus planning serves to decentralize the decisionmaking process. Schools determine how to improve student performance through collaboration. Together, principals, teachers, campus staff, parents, and community and business representatives assess the educational outcomes of students, determine performance objectives and strategies, and ensure that strategies are implemented and adjusted to improve student achievement for all students.

ing the production and implementation of their respective schools' campus improvement plans.[7]

In reality, NAS schools were not all that different from non-NAS schools in that common planning periods tended to be used similarly. At all schools in the district, teachers were given one weekly grade-level planning period to promote collaboration.

At NAS schools, schedules were arranged to allow for double planning periods. Teachers were to use this time to write curriculum, discuss projects, gather resources, and develop units. NAS teachers complained that though they were given more time to work with one another, in actuality, they were often impeded from doing so by having to discuss a variety of other issues typically district-generated. Planning time, too, was frequently curtailed in favor of addressing district issues. NAS teachers also reported not meeting at times to take care of such administrative business as paperwork, book-keeping, and testing. As one teacher stated:

> The paperwork has multiplied like ten-fold it seems like. Every time we turn around we have to do a paper. . . . I mean we have to write everything the kids are doing and where they are low, where they are not low, what they need, what they've done, how you addressed it, what still needs to be done. . . . There's always something coming from the . . . district office that we have to fill out. . . . Everyone is feeling overwhelmed.

TEACHER SUPPORT FOR THE NAS DESIGNS

Over the two school years we conducted our research, one indication of changes in NAS implementation came from an item that asked teachers how strongly they supported or opposed the NAS design team program in their school. In 1998, 54 percent of teachers indicated that they "strongly support a NAS design team program" in

---

[7]In accordance with district requirements, each school must include the following four sections in its Campus Improvement Planning Document: (1) the introduction; (2) needs assessment component; (3) goals, objectives, and strategies; and (4) activities and evaluations.

their schools, but this fell to 25 percent in 1999. The proportion of teachers indicating that they strongly opposed or somewhat opposed NAS designs in their school increased from 15 percent in 1998 to 43 percent in 1999.

Clearly, the central office played as active a role in initiating change across the district as did design teams in their select schools. The actions of the central office made it difficult for NAS teachers to view design implementation as a district priority. Consequently, these teachers were not able to fully commit to the ideas described in their respective designs' literature. Some feared that the NAS initiative, too, like many others that had been introduced over the years, would fade away in time. Furthermore, aspects of designs such as ELOB, MRSH, and Co-NECT overwhelmed many teachers. The task of writing curriculum was not an activity readily undertaken or easily accomplished by many, given their lack of time and experience.

During our interviews, teachers reported variation with respect to levels of design implementation within their schools. Implementation in individual classrooms depended in large part on teachers' feelings for designs, their willingness to invest time and energy, and their particular strengths and weaknesses. One teacher in our sample stated that within her school, differing levels of competency existed among teachers. The task of having to write curriculum "exacerbated the unevenness":

> There's always strengths and weaknesses, but when you have teachers filling dual roles of the writers of the curriculum and the implementers, then you compound whatever weaknesses you have. And also compounding strengths, that happens too.

Another teacher reported that within her school, some of her colleagues were more engaged in design implementation than others. In her words, "We have some who are very reluctant, who are barely doing anything. . . . Now slowly but surely they're coming around, but it's not at the same speed as a lot of others."

Other teachers stated:

> You have to have your commitment factor. Some people are very committed to it and other people are not, so that affects how you're going to implement it.

as far as some elements of Co-NECT, it's pretty basic and everybody has the same level. Now to the extreme of using the Internet sites or all those types of things, that would depend upon that individual staff member or grade level on what access they're going to be utilizing out there that's provided by Co-NECT. So I think there's some very beginning stages for everyone to get you started and then how far you take it beyond that, of course, is how much time or energy you have to spend in Co-NECT.

A number of teachers believed that NAS designs alone did little to help children who lacked solid academic foundations. Due in large part to other district activities that were pushed, some came to view designs as hands-on, project-oriented approaches to education that built *on*, not *up*, basic skills. One teacher at an ELOB school believed that her students needed more orderly classroom experiences, given that many came from "unstructured home environments."

> it would work probably better with a group of kids that are on grade level, that have a lot of self-control. . . . If they come from a home where there is no structure [and] they come into a classroom where there is no structure . . . that's the problem. But I really feel, and I might be wrong, that this works with a different population much better than what it has worked with our students.

Teachers at a Co-NECT school stated that their design units had to be "modified" to address their students' basic skills needs. At SFA/RW and MRSH schools, teachers expressed less doubt about the potential of NAS designs to bring about desired change in school achievement. This may have to do with the fact that their respective designs either gave them a curriculum to follow (SFA/RW) or topics to develop and standards to incorporate (MRSH).

In the next chapter, we focus specifically on the curriculum and instructional conditions in NAS and non-NAS classrooms. When examining these classroom conditions, it is important to remember the influences described of district, design teams, and school environments on NAS teachers' capacities to fully implement the instructional components of NAS designs.

Chapter Five

CLASSROOMS IMPLEMENTING NAS DESIGNS IN A REFORM-MINDED DISTRICT

As discussed in a previous chapter, the district introduced NAS designs as an overarching initiative for improving student achievement. Weary of the piecemeal practice of reform that had dominated the previous administration's efforts at school improvement, the superintendent partnered with New American Schools to push schools to comprehensively examine change from within. The central office also introduced NAS designs to its schools with hopes that each would sustain the reform effort. Simultaneously, the district began to critically examine the curriculum and instructional strategies its schools employed.

As late as the 1998–1999 school year, three years since most of our sample NAS schools had adopted designs, no campus had yet implemented its chosen design completely or purely—that is, as each is described in the design literature (http://www.newamericanschools. org/teams; Bodily, 2001). In part this had to do with the fact that most schools still were fairly new to their selected designs. In this chapter, we describe the classroom conditions in high-poverty, urban NAS and non-NAS classrooms to gain a better understanding of the progress of design implementation early on in the process. Specifically, we examine the overall curriculum changes that were occurring throughout the district during the course of this study and then describe the changes in classroom organization and instructional practices.

DISTRICT RESTRUCTURING OF THE CURRICULUM

Because students within the San Antonio school district were low performers on TAAS, district administrators wanted the district to do what it could to ensure its students' success. Believing that teachers had neither the expertise nor the time to learn and develop a sequential, standards-aligned curriculum across grade levels, the district took on this role full force. To meet the academic needs of its students, the district not only adopted particular research-based initiatives, over the years it also introduced its schools to specific instructional strategies.

By the 1998–1999 school year, not only were elementary schools, district wide, expected to schedule two 90-minute blocks of uninterrupted instructional time for reading and math, respectively, teachers were required to manage time within these blocks in prescribed ways. Though not to the same degree, the district structured language arts activities (spelling, grammar, and writing) as well, totaling approximately 70 minutes of instruction time per day. Thus, roughly four hours of instructional activities were mapped out for all the district's elementary school teachers to follow (SFA/RW teachers were exempt from the district reading program).

Mathematics

The district provided the most detailed guidance with respect to math. Teachers were given a pacing guide—that is, a highly prescriptive schedule that specified which lessons were to be covered during a given week. It was to be followed conscientiously. In fact district staff or school administrators periodically looked through math workbooks to ensure accountability.

> There's more of a lock and step way they [the district] want you to be. . . . We did Everyday Math last year, but now you have to have a date in which you play a game, and you have to have charts on the [walls]. It involves a lot of clerical tasks . . . that have been added, mandated. . . . We played the games last year, but now I have to go back there, and I have to put a date when I played the games. A lot of clerical things like that. . . . They'll come in and say, "Well, where's your math message." It's these little bitty things that when

you start to think of all the things, they add up. Any they make you feel as if you're being restricted. (Co-NECT)

for math we have people that come by. They would come in to check up in our math books to make sure we were on a certain page. . . . So we feel like if we miss one lesson in math and they come in to check and we haven't done it, then we'll be in trouble. So that kind of rushes us with the math. We don't get to teach to master it.

With the approach of TAAS, teachers reportedly put Everyday Math aside to focus on solving TAAS-formatted math problems. Because the district required that Everyday Math journals be periodically checked for completion, teachers found themselves planning "math-a-thons" to catch up after TAAS.

we have TAAS practice, which is three whole days we lose from teaching because we're doing the test. Then they [the district] mandate that you can't get behind, so we spend the rest of the next week trying to double up on our math. They [district personnel] come in . . . and check our journals.

Another source of difficulty for teachers was that Everyday Math as-sumed a certain level of background math knowledge which many students performing below grade level did not have. The teachers expressed that the program failed to remedy their students' lack of basic skills or understanding in that its spiraling approach to in-struction did not immediately teach to mastery. Concepts were in-troduced repeatedly, in greater depth each time, with the under-standing that *eventually* students would comprehend the material. According to one teacher:

I have nine students who are learning disabled. And I'm supposed to teach them . . . a math program that they may not be ready for because they don't have the foundation. . . .

Given that at many schools older students were introduced to Every-day Math not ever having been exposed to its terminology and strategies in earlier grades, teachers initially experienced difficulty with the program. After it had been in place for three years, they finally became comfortable enough with Everyday Math, making instruction easier. Ironically, it was then that all teachers in the district were given the opportunity to officially adopt this math program. In the spring of 1999, teachers voted against the Everyday Math in favor of Advantage Math, a math program more traditional in nature.

Finally, because math instruction tended to be very structured and time-consuming, teachers treated it as an activity in and of itself. That is, they rarely found ways to mesh math instruction with their design projects and/or activities.

> Whenever we write these units, we try to write a component for reading, language, science, social studies, everything. . . . And math is considered separate. In fact, we don't even have to write a math component into the unit. (MRSH)

> Math has nothing to do with Modern Red.

> I've been told in the math, I have to spend 90 minutes or more with Everyday Math. . . . so having to do that, a lot of times I just haven't always put the math component in [the expeditions], because I'm going to have to teach a math lesson anyhow.

> The Everyday Math we had, we were on a time schedule to finish so many lessons and it didn't matter whether that lesson went along with something we were doing in expeditions or not.

Reading and Language Arts

Though less prescriptive in nature than the math pacing guide, teaching plans for reading and language arts (called "Instructional Expectations and Learner Outcomes") were issued each grading period during the 1998–1999 school year. The district required that students read silently in class for 20 minutes every day. Students were expected to maintain a book log detailing their readings and thoughts about what they read. The teachers also were required to engage their students in daily "focus lessons" during which time they were to introduce reading strategies or skills (e.g., vocabulary, comprehension, text analysis, and reading strategies). Finally, teachers were expected to divide their students into three different level groups and hold reading circles for 20 minutes each. The district not only structured the time involved, it also suggested which activities be made available to students left on their own: listening centers, seatwork targeting specific reading skills, and/or silent reading.

During the 1998–1999 school year, having brought forth its instructional plans for math and reading, the Office of Curriculum and Instruction introduced its teachers to a detailed language arts guide. Students were required to write in their "read and respond journals" for several minutes every day after listening to their teachers read aloud. Their teachers were to provide them with 15 minutes of daily spelling instruction. Every week, students were expected to memorize lists of spelling words found in their district-issued textbook. They also were required to work on grammar for ten minutes each day in the form of "Daily Oral Language." Toward the end of the 1998–1999 school year, the district strongly encouraged classroom teachers at all grade school levels to incorporate learning centers into a portion of their language arts block.

> They [the district] want a certain way that we teach reading. . . . We now have a framework that says do 10 minutes of this, 15 minutes of this, 15 minutes of that, 30 minutes of this.

> The district gave us a very strict time line this year [1998–1999]. Up to the second almost. Ten minutes here, five minutes there, and you're out of there. . . . You have to do just 15 minutes silently, ten minutes in the journals. . . . And that's really affected a lot of the teaching.

Writing activities, too, were structured by the district. All fourth grade teachers in our sample found writing an especially taxing responsibility in light of the fact that their students faced the TAAS writing exam for the first time. Although students at all grade levels were expected to engage in some aspect of writing, most fourth grade teachers felt that they had no choice but to teach writing from scratch, given that these skills tended to be underdeveloped. In addition to introducing and practicing the process of writing (from brainstorming to drafting to editing), it was the responsibility of fourth grade teachers to ensure that their students be able to produce works written in different styles. Fourth grade students were expected to know how to write classificatory, narrative, how-to, and persuasive papers not only for their own good, but also for TAAS. Most of the NAS teachers we observed tried to incorporate writing as much as possible into their project work.

The district dictated the types of mini lessons to be incorporated into daily writing instruction as well as the amount of time to be spent. As the writing TAAS neared (February), however, several fourth grade teachers found the daily 35 minutes of practice and instruction to be too little. Consequently, during the winter months, more than half the fourth grade teachers we spoke with reported (or were observed) devoting significantly more time to writing.

The district's promotion of a varied assortment of instructional practices reflected both the back-to-basics movement as well as more progressive approaches to teaching. Some of these activities actually resembled aspects of NAS designs. For example, the structured reading time, ability-grouped reading circles, and read and response journal writings reflected elements of SFA. The provision of computers and printers in all classrooms, as well as the district's request that all teachers receive computer training and incorporate their newly acquired skills into lesson plans, reminded one of Co-NECT. The district's emphasis on standards, both the state's and their own, resembled MRSH. Center-work reflected aspects of ELOB. The NAS schools faced competing demands between the district initiatives and the implementation of NAS designs. As one teacher stated:

> You're told what to do and how to do it for reading. You're told that the spelling has to be done every day according to a spelling list that has nothing to do with whatever projects your students are working on. You're told what page and lesson to be on in math and math takes an hour and a half. . . . So everything's becoming very prescriptive. And everything has to tie into the process and the objectives on the process.

In the words of another teacher: "We're just here following. . . . That's what really hurt this year. It felt like we didn't have the ability to make instructional decisions. Everything is in its place. Do this. Do that."

Given the district's focus on promoting a variety of instructional approaches, what were the instructional conditions in NAS classrooms? Did these differ from those in non-NAS classrooms within a reform-minded district? In the sections that follow, we draw on our different sources of data to describe the early implementation of NAS designs in classrooms within high-poverty schools.

CLASSROOM ORGANIZATION

Many key items on the teacher survey focused on activities at the classroom level. Teachers were asked about skills they emphasized, instructional strategies they used, grouping practices within classrooms, assessments and grading criteria, instructional materials and technology. Before describing other instructional strategies, we begin with a view of average class size and grouping practices and then go on to examine differences found between NAS and non-NAS classrooms across a variety of classroom conditions and instructional practices. We highlight differences across 1998 and 1999 for our longitudinal sample of 40 teachers and bring information from our observations and interviews where appropriate.

Class Size

An important educational issue has been the class size in which students receive instruction (Bohrnstedt and Stecher, 1999; Stecher and Bohrnstedt, 2000; Grissmer, 1999). In general, teacher survey responses did not indicate clear distinctions between classrooms in NAS and non-NAS schools in terms of class size. Teachers were asked to indicate the number of students in their classrooms at the time they responded to the survey (late spring of 1998 and 1999). Overall, teachers in NAS and non-NAS elementary school classrooms had about 18 students, which is within the range for which class size reduction efforts have found positive effects on student achievement in the elementary grades (Grissmer, 1999). NAS teachers reported slightly smaller class sizes by about one or two students (Figure 5.1). This overall similarity between NAS and non-NAS classrooms is likely due to state policy on reducing class sizes (Texas Educational Agency, 1999).

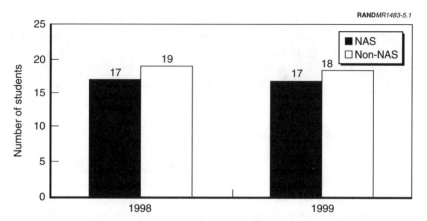

RAND*MR1483-5.1*

NOTE: Numbers are teacher-reported and based on a total sample size of 40 teachers—
26 NAS and 14 Non-NAS.

**Figure 5.1—Average Class Size in NAS and Non-NAS Schools,
Spring 1998 and 1999**

Grouping Practices

With respect to student grouping, each design articulates its own approach. The MRSH design endorses multiage, multiyear classroom
groupings with few pullouts. Within this environment, students can
be observed working individually as well as in a variety of groups,
depending on project. In Co-NECT schools, one also expects to see
multiage, multiyear arrangements. However, this design allows for
other grouping strategies as well—tracking being the one exception.
The ELOB design also does not endorse tracking. In addition to
mainstreaming special education students, it espouses looping.
Teachers are to stay with the same students for two to three years to
nurture relationships. One expects to see ELOB students working in
small groups. The SFA/RW design, unlike the other designs, openly
endorses the homogenous grouping of students by reading level.
However, students are to be assessed every eight weeks and reassigned as appropriate, providing a flexible use of grouping for instructional purposes. This way, students can receive the individual
attention they need.

Teachers in NAS classrooms tended to report using non-traditional grouping practices, although for the entire sample such practices were not widespread throughout any of the schools. Mean responses on survey items that addressed this issue (using a 6-point scale varying from does not describe my school to clearly describes my school) are provided in Table 5.1. By 1999, when considering whether grouping was flexible or was organized into block scheduling, NAS teachers tended to report in the middle of the 6-point scale (2.7 and 2.9, respectively). Compared with NAS teachers' reports on these indicators, non-NAS teachers scored somewhat lower. In addition, NAS teachers reported an increase between 1998 and 1999 when asked about whether their schools used more traditional ability grouping on a regular basis.

Our observations in NAS and non-NAS schools revealed that not all of the San Antonio NAS schools implemented the design team approaches to student grouping. And in fact, variation was observed within design by school as well. The SFA/RW schools strictly followed the guidelines laid out for them. They really had no choice, since the implementation of Success for All involved very specific actions. There was no room to deviate given the scripted curriculum and accompanying materials. At the two SFA/RW schools we followed, reading assessments, administered approximately every eight

Table 5.1

Teacher-Reported Means on the Extent to Which Grouping Practices Characterize NAS and Non-NAS Schools, Spring 1998 and 1999

	1998		1999	
	NAS	Non-NAS	NAS	Non-NAS
Student grouping is fluid, multiage, or multiyear	3.1	2.2	2.7	2.0
Students are organized into instructional groups using block scheduling for specific curricular purposes	3.5	2.4	2.9	2.6
Students in this school are grouped by achievement levels into high, middle, and/or remedial instructional groups on a regular basis	2.8	2.3	3.5	2.7

NOTE: Means are based on teacher reports in a total sample size of 40 teachers—26 NAS and 14 Non-NAS. Responses range from 1 "does not describe my school" to 6 "clearly describes my school."

weeks, determined how students should be grouped. In most cases, students tended to be similar in age. Teachers employed all the instructional strategies called for in their SFA lesson plans. Grouping strategies varied by activity. Not only did students learn as a class, they also worked individually and in small groups.

Only one of the ELOB schools in our sample practiced looping (teachers staying with the same group of students across school years). Both ELOB schools we visited, however, tended to place gifted and talented students together. The ELOB students we observed were given opportunities to work both independently and cooperatively. When asked to work together, students were given the option to work alone, which some took advantage of. However, when asked to work independently, students had no say. Relative to students exposed to SFA/RW, the ELOB students appeared to be less familiar with cooperative learning. When given the chance to work collaboratively, the students rarely solved problems together. They tended to work independently. Often, these students were put in small groups to assist or inspire one another as they worked on individual projects.

The grouping practices of the two Co-NECT schools we observed differed from one another. One engaged in looping; one did not. In the school that practiced looping, the fourth and fifth grade teachers collaborated quite extensively. However, they did not instruct each other's students. Desk arrangements varied by classroom. Students were observed working both individually and in small groups.

As for the MRSH schools we followed in San Antonio, no evidence of performance grouping, multiage classrooms, or multigrade teaching teams was observed. Looping, however, was practiced at one school. Students were not tracked by ability, but teachers did report that the gifted and talented students tended to be the responsibility of one teacher. The teachers at both MRSH schools periodically regrouped their students and rearranged desks as appropriate, but such changes tended to be socially based. Students were grouped differently as necessary throughout the day, but the groupings did not vary that dramatically. Students worked either independently or in small groups. They also learned as a whole class.

About six weeks prior to the TAAS, teachers at two of the NAS schools reported working with a variety of students. That is, grade-level teachers pooled their class lists and then divided all students by areas of weakness as determined by performance on the most recently administered TAAS simulation. Each grade-level teacher worked with one ability group for a set amount of time.

Overall, teachers in the NAS classrooms did tend to use more varieties of grouping practices than teachers in the non-NAS classrooms. Grouping practices were not consistent, however, among designs and schools.

INSTRUCTIONAL PRACTICES

We examined a variety of survey questions about both the skills students are expected to demonstrate and the particular instructional strategies teachers use in their classrooms. Since NAS designs tend to emphasize higher-order, analytic thinking skills over more basic skills, we might expect teachers in NAS classrooms to report lower levels of memorization and higher levels of other types of critical thinking skills (Bodilly, 2001). We sorted teacher responses about student tasks and teacher practices according to more conventional or reform-like categories of instruction. While some of the reports are based on teacher surveys, which may be subject to problems of response biases due to exposure to reform jargon (Mayer, 1999; Burstein et al., 1995), we believe the following comparisons are informative. Moreover, we also draw on our observational data, interviews with teachers, and examination of student work to further our understanding about what instructional practices occurred across elementary classrooms in the district.

CONVENTIONAL INSTRUCTIONAL PRACTICES

Figure 5.2 shows mean responses on a 4-point scale (from almost never to every lesson) in which teachers were asked, "How often do you have students memorize facts or problems?" Memorization tended to be emphasized more by non-NAS teachers, but only in 1998. The slight increase in NAS responses in 1999 may be due to the increased pressures schools were experiencing to switch to more basic skills instruction to prepare for the TAAS.

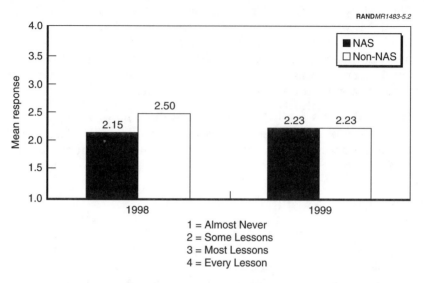

RAND*MR1483-5.2*

1 = Almost Never
2 = Some Lessons
3 = Most Lessons
4 = Every Lesson

NOTE: Means are based on teacher reports in a total sample size of 40 teachers—
26 NAS and 14 Non-NAS.

**Figure 5.2—Average Teacher Response for Having Students Memorize
Facts or Problems in the Typical Lesson in NAS and Non-NAS
Schools, Spring 1998 and 1999**

We also asked teachers to indicate how often they used particular instructional strategies in their classes, using a 5-point scale, ranging from never to almost every day. Responses from teachers in NAS and non-NAS schools varied only slightly in both years when it came to reporting on conventional instructional strategies such as:

- Work individually on written assignments/worksheets in class;

- Practice or drill on computational skills;

- Read textbooks or supplementary materials; and

- Work on next day's homework in class.

With the exception of the last item, well over 90 percent of all 40 teachers reported using these strategies at least once or twice a week.

Between 21 and 29 percent of teachers indicated having students work on their next day's homework in classes that often.

In general, teachers in the NAS schools indicated less reliance on more conventional instructional strategies than teachers in non-NAS schools. Teachers in non-NAS schools were much more likely to use conventional instructional strategies such as lecturing, administering a test over a full class period, and administering quizzes.

Reform-Like Instructional Practices

Teachers responded to several survey items asking about how often students were requested to demonstrate analytical and higher-order thinking skills, using a 4-point scale (from almost never to every lesson). We found few differences in NAS teachers' responses compared with non-NAS teachers when asked how often students use library sources, brainstorm ideas for written work, debate ideas, apply concepts or skills from earlier lessons, judge and critique their own and each others' work, reflect, relate the material to their life or their community, draft and redraft work, and work in teams toward a common goal.

Non-NAS teachers, on average, reported a higher degree of emphasis only on the item that asked about how often students "independently conduct and design their own research project." In both 1998 and 1999, 70 percent of non-NAS teachers reported having students conduct such projects in at least some lessons, compared with 60 percent in 1998 and 31 percent in 1999 for teachers in NAS classrooms. When we examined responses to this item in more detail, we found that in 1998, teachers in ELOB, Co-NECT, and to some extent MRSH (73 percent) indicated having students conduct such projects in at least some lessons. Fewer teachers in RW classrooms (36 percent) reported use in at least some lessons, which likely reflects RW not emphasizing project-based learning within its design. By 1999, when emphasis on NAS designs was generally decreasing, most teachers in all the NAS classrooms indicated that this instructional strategy was "almost never" used.

Another set of survey items measuring instructional strategies was used to construct a composite for reform-like instructional practices.

Responses from two scales were standardized—to indicate (1) how often teachers used the instructional strategies with this class (a 5-point scale ranging from never to almost every day) and (2) how often teachers had students demonstrate skills (a 4-point scale ranging from almost never to every lesson). The following items were included in the reform composite:[1]

- Have students listen to an outside speaker/expert;

- Have students perform research projects;

- Use manipulatives to demonstrate a concept;

- Have students work with manipulatives;

- Have small groups work on problems to find a joint solution;

- Have the whole class discuss solutions developed in small groups;

- Have students work on problems for which there is no obvious method or solution;

- Have students represent and analyze relationships using tables and graphs;

- Have students respond to questions or assignments that require writing at least a paragraph;

- Have students keep a journal;

- Summarize main points of today's lesson;

- Have students work on projects in class;

- Have students explain their reasoning; and

- Have students represent and analyze relationships using tables, graphs, or charts.

Teachers' responses for this reform-like instructional composite are provided in Figure 5.3. While the average use of reform-like instructional practices increased for NAS and non-NAS teachers between

---

[1]The alpha reliability for this composite was 0.77 for both 1998 and 1999. The range of correlations for the individual items was 0.17 to 0.20 in both years.

1998 and 1999, teachers in NAS schools reported higher levels than their counterparts in non-NAS schools. For example, in 1999, 54 percent of NAS teachers reported using practices in the reform-like composite at least once or twice a week compared with 36 percent of non-NAS teachers.

Given the unique features of designs and their respective emphases on student work products, one would reasonably expect to see differences in classroom appearance, setup, and student work displays across design schools. While such displays are a simple way that teachers can give the impression of superficial compliance to implementing a reform, we found even these displays were less apparent in the second year than the first year of our study. In the first year, design elements were often clearly identifiable. In MRSH classrooms, standards were posted next to student work. Word walls and team score sheets were posted in SFA/RW classrooms. Rich classroom libraries were found in Co-NECT classrooms and student work linked to themes and a multidisciplinary perspective was posted in

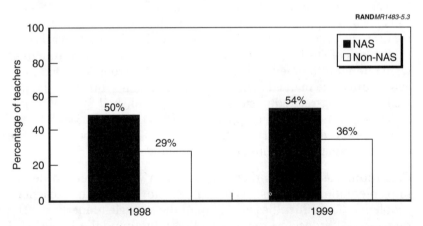

NOTE: Percentages are based on a total sample size of 40 teachers—26 NAS and 14 Non-NAS.

Figure 5.3—Percentage of Teachers Who Reported Using Reform-Like Instructional Practices at Least Once or Twice a Week in NAS and Non-NAS Schools, Spring 1998 and 1999

hallways and classrooms. Displayed throughout ELOB classrooms were expedition themes, student-developed rubrics, and drafts and re-drafts of student writing.

In year two of our study, the growing influence of the central office on classroom affairs was reflected in the other types of postings found on classroom walls. Across our sample schools, identical posters outlining the writing and reading processes, math definitions, and district-developed rubrics were commonly found taped to classroom walls. In every classroom, word walls were found as well as postings of student work on bulletin boards. Classrooms across our sample looked alike in other ways as well. The district provided all classrooms with six computers and at least one printer. All computers were loaded with the same programs. The same trade books were found in every room. In most classrooms, desks were commonly arranged in clusters of four to six. Teachers across schools reportedly rearranged students quite regularly to enable classmates to get to know one another.

One could tell that classrooms were part of given designs only because teachers advertised this fact through posters. In MRSH classrooms various standards tended to be posted on bulletin boards next to displays of student work. In ELOB classrooms design principles were often found taped to walls. Co-NECT classrooms tended to be less distinctively marked. The selection of student work on display as well as reading-related posters clearly distinguished SFA/RW classrooms from the rest. The appearance of classrooms as well as the work displayed revealed teachers' efforts to comply with both the district's demands and those of their selected designs.

Classroom observations revealed a schism with respect to design implementation. The designs per se were not the source of teachers' problems. The difficulties arose out of the struggle to merge district demands with design practices while maintaining the integrity of designs. All teachers indicated in their talks with us that they perceived passing TAAS scores to be the bottom line. With this in mind, the teachers were left on their own to figure out how to incorporate district initiatives into their lesson plans in the spirit of their designs. To determine whether NAS teachers and students actually interacted with each other and subject materials in ways reflective of design teams' curricular and instructional theories, classroom activities were examined with care.

Use of Assessments

NAS's ultimate goal is to help schools realize improved student performance. In San Antonio, the TAAS is the preeminent measure of student performance. Clearly, it was very important to the district and its schools that students perform respectably on this standardized test. As in many urban school districts, San Antonio schools functioned in a high-stakes testing environment. Given this climate, the district assumed much of the responsibility for assuring the accountability of its schools and teachers by imposing a set of instructional standards and practices across the board—regardless of the existence of NAS designs at its schools. Moreover, teachers focused on reinforcing basic math and reading skills in their efforts to prepare students for TAAS.

Teachers from different design schools consistently remarked that with the approach of TAAS, instruction narrowed to honing tested skills. They questioned whether the instructional approaches espoused by their respective designs (e.g., project-based and interdisciplinary) alone could bring about test score increases. In the words of one teacher whose school dropped the design at the start of what would have been its third year, "There are some faculty members who bemoan the loss of their love [the design]. But I think all of us saw that it wasn't getting us where we needed to be when the requirement here is having a certain level of performance on the TAAS test."

As described in the previous chapter, teachers reported that TAAS preparation was a matter of practice and familiarizing students with test format. Given the district's numbers of students performing below grade level, it was important to them that they directly address tested skills. Teaching students how to take the TAAS was just as important to teachers as reviewing the skills to be tested. Such an assessment system within a high-stakes accountability environment does not fit well with most of the design teams' approaches (except SFA/RW), even though each team expresses a desire to work with whatever local assessment is in place (Bodilly, 2001).

No design was developed solely to produce high standardized test scores. Each design in fact promotes its own methods of assessment. The ELOB design calls for authentic assessment, including performance-based exhibitions, student portfolios, and student self-assessments. Student work products are to be shared with the community to ensure a certain quality of work and to encourage support. The Co-NECT design relies on a mix of assessments and portfolios to judge student achievement. Teachers use exemplar products that provide models and rubrics that explicitly describe the characteristics of varying levels of quality to encourage students to set goals and measure progress. The MRSH design, like Co-NECT, also relies on various assessments. Schools are required to use MRSH-developed tests to measure student performance and individual student contracts to measure progress toward standards. The SFA/RW design team uses a formal assessment at least every eight weeks to reassign students to reading groups. In addition, it endorses informal assessments to monitor individual progress.

Teachers across the various NAS schools reported using a variety of assessment measures. These ranged from observations to student work assessments to objective paper and pencil tests. All teachers made some use of rubrics. The district encouraged this and even provided teachers with several rubrics to use. In compliance with district policy, teachers also regularly administered spelling, math, and reading tests, as well as year-end reading and math tests.

The teachers at the MRSH schools we observed used rubrics to assess their students' projects. One teacher developed multiple-choice tests to assess her students' knowledge. At both schools, methods of assessment varied by subject. At neither school was there mention of watershed assessments or individual education compacts.

The Co-NECT teachers we spoke with also used district-established rubrics to some extent. None felt entirely comfortable with the process, however. With respect to Co-NECT projects, teachers seemed to apply different criteria depending on assignment type. There appeared to be no obvious measures of assessment in place. The Co-NECT teachers we observed did not put as much time into developing assessment tools as they did into planning units. Students were rarely shown exemplary work. Nor were the grading criteria explained to them up front.

At the ELOB schools we observed, the practice of assessment appeared to change greatly from the spring of 1998 to the spring of 1999. In the first year, students developed and applied their own rubrics and re-drafted their work. But, in the second year, teachers and students were not seen reexamining graded assignments or discussing ways to improve upon them. Nor did there appear to be any evidence of reflection on the quality of student work. Rubrics were used at times to grade student work, but it is not clear how consistently. The rubrics used by ELOB teachers tended to be those developed by other outside experts. The teachers at both ELOB schools we followed mentioned that they really were unclear as to how their design defined good quality work.

> Show us what a good product is. Is this a good product? Give us an [example of] authentic product. Is a book an authentic product? . . . What is an authentic product? What does that look like?

Most MRSH and Co-NECT teachers we talked with also expressed the need to see examples of quality products and/or teacher-developed units:

> If I can see it, see a product . . . then I get an idea. But just hearing it, I can't picture that. (Co-NECT)

> I would like to see how does it look whenever a good unit is being taught. (MRSH)

The SFA/RW teachers we spoke with were only familiar with SFA. Given its scripted approach to reading, the practice of assessment was not an issue for SFA/RW teachers. At both SFA/RW schools, reading assessments were administered about every eight weeks to determine students' reading levels. Based on their results, students were regrouped as necessary. Reading teachers used team score sheets to record their students' grades on SFA assignments. The score sheet enabled them to chart their students' progress over time.

On the teacher survey, respondents were asked to indicate the importance of varying types of assessment instruments using a 4-point scale (from not very important to very important). The only assessment that teachers in NAS schools rated as being important was the use of student portfolios. In general, non-NAS teachers tended to indicate higher levels of importance on most assessments used, including multiple-choice and essay tests (whether developed by the teacher, an outside source, or found within a unit or book), completion of homework, student work, open-ended problems, individual projects/reports, performance tasks or events, and standardized test results. Teachers in both NAS and non-NAS schools responded similarly with respect to the importance of assessing student participation in class and group projects/reports.

Use of Instructional Materials

Little variation was found between NAS and non-NAS teachers in the use of instructional materials. Both groups of teachers tended to use a variety of materials fairly frequently in their classrooms, including textbooks, literature books, workbooks, computers, calculators, manipulatives, audio-visual equipment, games, lab equipment, and library materials.

NAS teachers were more likely than non-NAS teachers to report that inadequate instructional materials hindered student achievement (see Figure 5.4). For example, in 1998, 35 percent of NAS teachers reported that instructional materials hindered students' academic success either moderately or greatly compared with 21 percent of non-NAS teachers. For these same teachers, 16 percent of NAS teachers and 7 percent of non-NAS teachers reported that inadequate instructional materials posed a barrier to students' academic success in 1999. It is likely that this overall decline was due to the extensive curricular programs (mathematics, reading, language arts) being implemented district wide.

In the first year of our study, our classroom observations revealed that the use of instructional materials varied greatly among the NAS designs. While non-NAS and MRSH students were seen using textbooks, traditional literature, and pencil and paper, students in Co-NECT and ELOB schools were observed accessing various other materials during project time, including reference books, the Internet, and sometimes multimedia software. They also left the room to gather resources from the library or other classrooms. During the SFA block, SFA/RW students used the SFA workbooks and trade books supplied by the design.

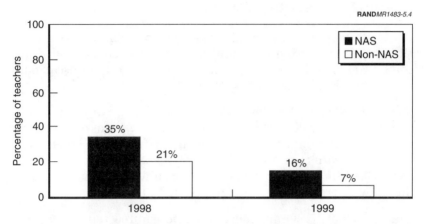

NOTE: Percentages are based on a total sample size of 40 teachers—26 NAS and 14 Non-NAS.

Figure 5.4—Percentage of Teachers Who Reported That Inadequate Instructional Materials Moderately or Greatly Hindered Students' Academic Success in NAS and Non-NAS Schools, Spring 1998 and 1999

By the second year, materials used for instructional purposes tended to be more similar across schools, regardless of design presence. The technology available in classrooms was similar, for example. Students across the district read many of the same books and engaged in tasks that required little more than pencil and paper. Even the SFA classrooms contained the same reading materials as the other district schools, although they were not used during the reading block. Given that the district required all schools to adopt the same math curriculum and employ specific instructional strategies in the areas of reading and language arts, it is not all that surprising that the materials found in classrooms tended to be more alike than different. However, although the materials were similar, they were not always utilized in the same way by all campuses. For example, one of our Co-NECT schools employed the available technology more readily than most other campuses.

EXAMPLES OF STUDENT WORK

The work students produced also tended to look alike across schools. However, a close examination of the work collected revealed that some teachers more so than others espoused an interdisciplinary, reform-minded instructional approach.

So that RAND could better understand the nature of student work assigned over the course of one year, teachers were asked to submit examples of student work every three months or so. No criteria were established with regard to work submissions. The teachers simply were asked to provide examples of typical work assignments produced by several of their randomly selected students.[2]

Quite possibly the submitted work was not entirely representative of all student assignments made by a given teacher; nonetheless, an analysis of the student pieces revealed the types of activities assigned by each of the teachers in our sample. Each piece of work was coded according to several variables, such as content area, nature of assignment (e.g., journal entry, essay, etc.), as well as whether the piece provided evidence of use of standards, technology, cooperative learning, connection to an overall theme, drafts, rubrics, or other individual design elements. In addition, the degree with which students had to apply skills to culminating projects or themes was noted. Overall, the student work revealed the use of a uniform fourth grade curriculum across schools within San Antonio. For example, in social studies, students across NAS and non-NAS schools studied Texas history, including such topics as regions, Indians, exploration, missions, settlements, and tall tales.

Although the submissions were similar in content and skills emphasized, they revealed that teachers did not present the curriculum in the same ways. For cxample, some teachers made efforts to cover multiple objectives simultaneously by having students write biographies about famous people from Texas history. Other teachers allowed students to write biographies on any famous person, past or present.

---

[2]RAND randomly selected one-quarter of the students in each class every three months. Once a student was selected, his or her name was removed from the class roster.

One pattern that emerged was a tendency of NAS teachers to incorporate the practice of reading and writing skills whenever they could. Thus, when covering a social studies topic, or on rare occasions a science lesson, for example, they had their students activate the reading process and write how-to, classificatory, persuasive, and/or narrative papers. By contrast, non-NAS teachers tended to use more traditional and compartmentalized strategies to teach social studies and science, such as fill-in-the-blank questions at the end of a social studies chapter (see Tables 5.2 and 5.3 for examples of lesson plans).

Although design teachers made efforts to integrate district- or state-required content material into their units of study, they did not consistently engage their students in interdisciplinary work. Many tended to endorse a more traditional instructional style some of the time, teaching subjects as discrete disciplines and relying on worksheets and textbook assignments. In some ways, they were encouraged to do so. For example, teachers were required to calculate report card grades for each subject; moreover, they were

Table 5.2

Example of a Conventional Lesson Plan

Language Arts	Math	Social Studies	Science
TAAS Master p. 38 Write a story about the day the Snowman came to life, listing ideas	Students will locate places on an atlas map, solve problems in math box 51, and record information about latitude and longitude. *Everyday Math Workbooks* pp. 236–238	*A Paradise Called Texas*—Use Reading Process to gather information about the German culture in Texas for a report to be presented in class	Students will make and use a book about magnetism—AIMS Lesson. After creating the book, reading and discussing info on magnets, students will experiment with magnets.
Give Spelling pre-test on unit 15 Vocabulary focus, *Beat the Story Drum*, p. 227			
Test Ready pp. 33 & 34	Student journal pp. 145 & 146		
Independent Reading, pp. 227–247 using the reading process & do Sum It Up	Study Links 50 & 51 *World Tour Guide Book* and record sheets 1, 5–7		

Table 5.3

**Example of a Lesson Plan Consistent with Reform-Like Orientation
of a NAS Design**

Title: Europe in the Middle Ages

Abstract: This unit focuses on the development of civilization during the European Middle Ages from 400 A.D. to 1500 A.D. The social studies component is research-based and includes geography, feudalism, chivalry, timelines, and the study of important people. The language arts focus is on writing and dialect. Math includes measurement and construction of castles. Reading incorporates myths, legends, and an understanding of real and fictional characters. Science is included with the study of hygiene and diseases. Art and drama are fully executed throughout the entire unit with the production of a play and the creation of artifacts.

MRSH Core Knowledge Sequence: World Civilization for the fourth grade.

Note: the teacher goes on to outline 12 lessons in the unit

---

expected to follow state and district-mandated curricular and instructional guidelines by subject. Teachers had the latitude to tie subjects together, but the constraints within which they operated tended to limit their vision.

As revealed earlier, teachers across design schools reported that they found it difficult to integrate Everyday Math lessons with other subjects. Thus, they taught it as a subject in and of itself and our analysis of student work was consistent with the teacher challenges expressed during interviews and observations.

In general, the SFA/RW and non-NAS schools modeled a traditional approach to instruction, focusing on compartmentalized skill exercises. They utilized worksheets and textbook assignments as prescribed by SFA. The student work submitted by ELOB and Co-NECT teachers reflected a more interdisciplinary unit-based approach to instruction and showed more evidence of contemporary teaching practices (e.g., the use of rubrics, cooperative grouping, and integrated technology). One of our Co-NECT schools, more so than the other, however, reflected a more traditional approach to teaching. The MRSH schools employed a mix of strategies including project-oriented work that incorporated a variety of skills in the process.

Use of Technology for Instructional Purposes

Since NAS designs such as Co-NECT and MRSH tend to emphasize the use of technology in the classroom, two survey items addressed this issue. As shown in Figure 5.5, compared with NAS teachers, those in non-NAS schools indicated slightly higher levels of technology being used as an integrated classroom resource. In both sets of schools teachers reported that technology use declined from 1998 to 1999, despite a district-wide effort to support the use of computers in all elementary schools.

The second item focused more on technology use in schools than in classrooms. As shown in Figure 5.6, teachers in NAS and non-NAS schools reported a decline in technology being used to manage curriculum, instruction, and student progress. By 1999, 12 percent of NAS teachers agreed that such use of technology described their school, while 21 percent of non-NAS teachers agreed.

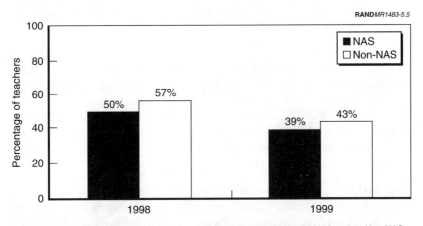

RAND*MR1483-5.5*

NOTE: Percentages are based on a total sample size of 40 teachers—26 NAS and 14 Non-NAS.

Figure 5.5—Percentage of Teachers Who Reported That Technology Was Clearly an Integrated Classroom Resource in NAS and Non-NAS Schools, Spring 1998 and 1999

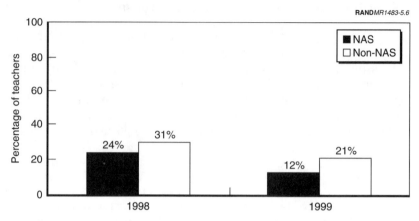

RAND*MR1483-5.6*

NOTE: Percentages are based on a total sample size of 40 teachers—26 NAS and 14 Non-NAS.

Figure 5.6—Percentage of Teachers Who Reported That Technology Was Definitely Used to Manage Curriculum, Instruction, and Student Progress in NAS and Non-NAS Schools, Spring 1998 and 1999

The decrease in teacher-reported use of technology in both schools and classrooms could in part be explained by the increased demands on teacher time to comply with the district's math, reading, and language arts initiatives. The structure mandated by the district for teaching these subjects was time-consuming and fairly rigid and may have decreased the opportunities for teachers to incorporate technology into instruction.

Few indications of the use of technology were seen during our classroom observations. Computers were primarily used by students to type essays and reports. Occasionally, we saw students take reading tests on the computers. Once in a while students were observed playing educational games or researching topics on the Internet. Most of the time, however, the computers were not in use during classroom observations.

Comments made by several NAS teachers during interviews also indicate that technology use was decreasing due to several factors. All the teachers we spoke with reported that there are lots of problems with computers and printers in the classrooms. Many of the computers were outdated and did not have the capacity to run the latest educational software available. Many were not connected to the Internet. Obtaining supplies, such as ink for the printers, and getting repairs done were often slow processes.

Some of the teachers mentioned training problems. Not all teachers were comfortable with computers. Most of the training available for teachers was offered after school and it was left up to the teachers to take it upon themselves to sign up for the courses. Teachers expressed that many did not have the time or the means to practice what they had learned in their training sessions.

One teacher pointed out that many of her fourth grade students were reading at a second grade level. Many students in the classrooms we visited were struggling readers. For such students, it is not always easy to work independently on computers.

TEACHER-REPORTED EFFECTS OF REFORM

On our surveys we asked NAS and non-NAS teachers whether the implementation of their schools' respective NAS design had positive effects on their professional work lives and on their students.

Teacher Reports of NAS Design Effects on Teaching and Learning

The school improvement composite was comprised of several items asking about the extent to which the NAS design had positive or negative effects on individual teachers':[3]

- Teaching;

- Professional growth;

---

[3]The teacher-reported effects composite was comprised of items on a 7-point scale (from great deal of negative effect to great deal of positive effect). The alpha reliability for this composite was 0.93 in 1998 and 0.96 in 1999. The range of correlations for the individual items was 0.46 to 0.85 in 1998 and 0.58 to 0.86 in 1999.

- Job satisfaction;
- Students' achievement;
- Students' enthusiasm for learning;
- Classroom curriculum; and
- Students' engagement in learning.

In both survey years, a substantial proportion of teachers in the NAS schools (83 percent in 1998 and 88 percent in 1999) attributed positive effects of the designs on these aspects of their work lives and on their students.

Few teachers felt that their style of teaching had dramatically shifted as a result of design training. Differences in the way teachers approached curriculum, however, were cited as a positive consequence of design implementation. Several teachers reported that they now engaged in much more research to prepare lessons and plan activities. The designs forced them to study topics and gain new content knowledge and a reliance on worksheets and textbooks.

At one of our Co-NECT schools, a teacher reported that because of the design, she became more aware that she needed to involve the community in her students' education and thus made a greater effort to get parents or "some kind of outside influence" into her classroom. Another teacher at a different Co-NECT school stated that the design led him to think more deeply about subject matter:

> When we plan, when we look at things, you look at them . . . much broader, more in-depth. And you're just not dealing with surface things because you really want to get involved in the product in what you're doing. Also, you find yourself pulling and researching more as a teacher, trying to find out more . . . about information, using the Internet to get a website and things like books and things like that. . . . And I think it's expanded what we teach.

At this school, teachers also cited increased technology use as a positive consequence of design implementation and training. Teachers were taught how to work computers and use them in their classrooms. According to those we spoke with, before Co-NECT, computers just sat there all day, "not being used."

Teachers at our MRSH schools remarked:

> I like the standards because they focus me. They show me exactly what I'm doing. . . . We used to just come in and teach a unit and hope for the best, you know. . . . And now it's much more focused. . . . Teaching is more focused. The principal knows what we're doing. Everybody knows what we're doing, if we have all the same focus.

> The greatest advantage to the school the design brings is that a lot of teachers who sit back and give worksheets can no longer do that, and I think that worksheets are taboo around here now. So I think it's made a lot of lazy teachers less lazy.

According to a teacher at an ELOB school, much of the training she received "raised a consciousness or awareness in (her) to better allow (her) to teach to the whole child, instead of just to academic flaws." Teachers at our other ELOB school reported that as a result of having the design in place, they noticed some improvement in their students' oral skills. Additionally, the design led them to engage their students in more group work and research.

Teachers at both SFA/RW schools we visited reported that they found it really advantageous to work with children at the same reading level. SFA enabled teachers to "focus on where the kids were actually reading and take them from there and fill in some of the gaps." At one of our SFA/RW schools, teachers stated that their students were reading more on their own as a result of the reading program. A teacher at the other SFA/RW school in our sample reported that several of her colleagues utilized the SFA reading strategies when teaching subjects that involved reading.

Over half of the NAS teachers reported their school had generally improved over the last three years, but by 1999 about half of the non-NAS teachers also reported such general improvements. When considering effects of NAS designs on teachers' professional life (teaching and professional growth) and student learning and engagement, NAS teachers tended to be quite positive. The mixed picture may be due to NAS teachers teaching in challenged schools with low-achieving students and having high expectations for student progress in the skill areas.

OVERARCHING THEMES

Analysis of responses to the survey revealed few differences in teacher perceptions of instructional environments between NAS and non-NAS schools. Some differences were evident. For example, teachers in NAS schools reported instructional strategies and class-room practices that could be categorized as reform-like, rather than conventional. In other areas, fewer differences were found. Teachers in non-NAS schools indicated more frequent use of traditional assessment instruments with their students. Both groups reported similar use of instructional materials, though more teachers in NAS than non-NAS schools perceived inadequate materials to be a problem. Use of technology in the classroom was more prevalent in non-NAS schools, but schoolwide use of technology was more prevalent in NAS schools.

The more substantial differences shown here, however, were not between NAS and non-NAS schools, but between 1998 and 1999, which is likely a reflection of the dramatic level of change within the district itself.

As shown in the last chapter, by the end of 1999, NAS teachers reported a substantial shift in their perceptions indicating little support and stronger opposition to NAS design team programs when compared with their perceptions a year earlier. Yet, this same group of teachers expressed relatively more positive views about the impact of NAS in both general and design-specific terms. These contradictory results could be attributed to changes in district administration and the emphasis on accountability and TAAS. Data collected in teacher focus groups, interviews, and classroom observation give more detail on the process of change in the district and teacher attitudes toward NAS and provide explanation and a context for the survey results described here. Perhaps the most influential factor that posed a barrier to sustained, meaningful NAS design implementation was the high-stakes assessment to which schools were held accountable. How the designs fit this accountability system was open to question. Yet, district personnel and teachers seemed to have little time to let this question be resolved. The result was more district initiatives aimed at changing teaching and learning that would be reflected by TAAS scores. The NAS designs were but a part of this mix of educational reforms.

District initiatives compromised the essence of designs by forcing the reduction of each to blocks of time. Teachers reported "doing Co-NECT" and "getting to ELOB and MRSH" upon completing such activities as daily oral language drill, journal writing, reading, and math. To be able to meet the demands of both district and design, teachers had little alternative but to turn their respective designs "on and off," depending on task. Often, this meant that teachers taught the design almost as a separate subject after completing reading, writing, and math lessons. In practice, the designs came to mean project time to students. The emphases on standards made this less the case at MRSH schools. In the second year of the study, when the district prescribed more instructional strategies, the new strategies took time away from engaging in design-related interdisciplinary projects.

The teachers did not feel that their designs necessarily competed with district initiatives, rather ideas regarding which to prioritize were what clashed. They found it difficult to actually integrate the ideas coming from both sources. This struggle was made manifest as one sat in classrooms and observed instruction. Not only was it clear that teachers turned designs on and off, most striking was that, by the second year of our study, regardless of whether schools were non-NAS or had in place Co-NECT, ELOB, MRSH, or SFA/RW, one saw similar instruction taking place.

Almost every teacher began his/her day with a daily oral language drill. All teachers taught the reading process and had students write in their "read and respond journals." All teachers employed Everyday Math. All students were taught spelling out of the same district-issued spelling books. All teachers reviewed specific TAAS skills and referred by name to key TAAS objectives. All fourth graders were taught four types of writing via the writing process.

Because teachers referred to state standards when developing design units, one saw students across design schools engage in similar activities and study identical topics. In Co-NECT, ELOB, and MRSH schools, various instructional activities centered on Texan Native Americans, for example, were observed during the 1998–1999 school year.

Interestingly, though introduced as design-inspired projects, several identical activities were performed across different design schools. In Co-NECT and ELOB schools, for example, the students wrote stories, using pictographs, on wrinkled brown paper shaped to resemble animal skins. In ELOB and MRSH schools, students constructed a variety of three-dimensional dwellings inhabited by native Texans.

In MRSH schools, teachers got together to develop instructional plans guided by the state, drawing from design and state standards as well as Core Knowledge. In ELOB schools, too, teachers developed expeditions around district mandates and Texas's education standards. Additionally, they derived inspiration from their ten design team principles, incorporating as many as they could into their lessons. Expeditions were planned to promote active student involvement and to nurture oral language skills. Co-NECT teachers, like the others, also developed curriculum based on state standards. The outcome differed only in that their lessons tended to make more use of technology. However, this observation, too, varied by school. One Co-NECT school more so than another in San Antonio tended to utilize computers to engage in research, produce hyper-studio reports, and type up written work. Students scanned photographs into their computers and tried to utilize the technological equipment they had available (e.g., digital camera and camcorder). However, even at this school, plans often derailed due to equipment failure.

The implementation of SFA/RW in San Antonio differed from the other three designs in that SFA/RW schools opted to implement only one aspect of the design: Success for All. This decision tended to ease the pressure that teachers at other design schools felt to "fit" design elements into their days. Given that SFA is a highly structured, prescribed reading program, an academic area of critical importance to the district, teachers in SFA/RW schools expressed greater confidence in their progress and degree of implementation than their colleagues at other design schools. By electing to adopt only SFA, implementation was made less challenging given its limited nature.

Clearly, district-issued curricular and instructional strategies regarding reading, language arts, and math limited the ability of teachers to develop units, expeditions, and lessons as described in their respective design literature. Moreover, because the schools were obligated to use the same math curriculum and engage in 90 minutes of uninterrupted math and reading instruction and 70 or so minutes of language arts activity, teachers tended to develop design units around social studies/science topics. Design activities were frequently scheduled for the afternoon.

Due to time constraints during the school day, teachers across the various design schools also revealed that they tended not to complete their units or expeditions as planned. So many unaccounted factors interrupted the flow of their "units" that time was lost. Because time was of the essence, teachers tended to move on to different units without producing final culminating products.

Instead of NAS designs guiding curriculum and instruction, it appears that the district and state initiatives directed the educational mission of all schools. TAAS success was obviously the major driving force behind all this. The district's influence was clearly revealed in the conversations we had with teachers, which explain many of our survey results showing few differences between NAS and non-NAS teachers. Regardless of design adoptions, teachers across the various San Antonio schools tended to voice the same frustrations. As previously stated, limited school hours and demands on teacher time were repeatedly discussed at all schools. Teachers frequently mentioned their difficulty trying to "fit" all district and design activities into any one school day. Teachers remarked that the emphasis on TAAS tended to stifle their creativity. They were given little opportunity to devise their own ways to meet the needs of their students.

All teachers expressed their annoyance at having to devote energy and time to seemingly petty activities, for example, checking students' math and writing journals for dates and times. They expressed that full-blown design implementation was difficult to accomplish given the variety and frequency of interruptions experienced throughout the year. At the beginning of the 1998–1999 school year, for example, teachers across schools were asked to attend district-sponsored workshops and/or training during the school day at least once a week. This was a source of much trouble. Being away tended to mean that students fell behind. Other interruptions reported by teachers included: TAAS simulations; preparation for TAAS; meetings called after school (often unexpectedly) to discuss district initiatives, taking time away from teachers to organize their classrooms and plan lessons; the introduction of district initiatives during teacher planning periods; the strict math pacing guide; the required administration of periodic math tests; and the paperwork required to document classroom activities.

> the district's programs come before design. That's the way it is.

> We've got to get the kids prepared for [TAAS]. So we're taking the time out to do that, to get the kids ready for it and we're operating in two different mindsets. . . .

> I don't know where our direction is at. I know that the district is becoming more and more a top-down situation where we're told this is what the reading is going to look like. When district staff walk in, they want to see the reading done in a certain way.

Our interviews revealed that though the district was supportive both financially and philosophically of NAS designs in its schools, it unwittingly hindered design implementation at all schools (except SFA/RW schools) by establishing an ever-growing presence in the daily classroom affairs of its teachers. The paucity of communication between the district and design teams failed to create the kind of supportive operating environment called for by NAS. Moreover, the limited communication between teachers and their respective design representatives served to weaken implementation as well. Not knowing how to integrate central office initiatives with design aspects, teachers tended to compromise designs by selecting and modifying only those elements that could coexist with district actions.

> I just think that [the district] is trying to do too many things. Maybe they feel that our schools are very low so they are doing all these other things without really giving us a chance to test it. . . . They are doing all these things without realizing that it's overkill. It's way too much.

Understanding the relationships between instructional practices and student achievement is important for understanding schooling processes and school improvement strategies (Klein et al., 2000; Gamoran et al., 1995; Oakes et al., 1992). Despite the similarities across the district in instructional conditions and the press of district reading and mathematics initiatives and the marginalization of NAS designs, it is worth exploring the relationships between instructional conditions and student achievement on the TAAS reading and mathematics tests as well as an independent open-ended reading assessment (Stanford-9). It is to this that we turn in the next chapter, first examining relationships in all the fourth grade classrooms and students, and second in the sample of classrooms and students for which RAND gathered additional survey information on classroom conditions and supplemental achievement scores.

Chapter Six

EFFECTS OF INSTRUCTIONAL CONDITIONS ON STUDENT ACHIEVEMENT

The ultimate aim of school reform efforts and implementation of NAS designs is to substantially improve student performance. In this chapter we turn to a quantitative analysis of test scores and examine the relative impact of factors influencing student performance. The empirical models constructed allow for an exploratory analysis of classroom effects of reform in a low-performing school district. Moreover, at the height of design implementation in San Antonio, curricular differences between NAS and non-NAS schools were evident. Here we explore the possibility of differences in student achievement through a comparison of conditions within NAS and non-NAS classrooms, taking into account the nesting of students within classrooms within schools. What follows is not a test of NAS design effects per se, because schools and classrooms were at the early stages in implementation. Rather, we focus on whether differences in instructional conditions are related to student achievement, net of other student, classroom, and school factors.[1] Particularly, we are interested in whether reform-like instructional conditions are related to student achievement because these are the practices that are consistent with what NAS design teams are attempting to

---

[1]It is important to note that while we examine mathematics achievement, the specific curriculum (Everyday Mathematics) being implemented was likely the primary driver of test scores, not the other reforms being implemented. Yet, it is informative to examine subjects other than reading to explore the effects of general instructional conditions on student achievement.

promote. Since these instructional practices had to vie for classroom time in the wake of district mandates, the effects of reforms may also be muted in this sample.

Several recent studies have contributed to the growing empirical work connecting reform-like practices, or authentic pedagogy, to student achievement. For example, Marks, Newmann, and Gamoran (1996) found that authentic pedagogy had a positive and significant relationship to student achievement in math and social studies as measured by student work assessment. Puma et al. (1997) found that an emphasis on reading comprehension and the development of writing skills and appreciation were positively related to student achievement as measured by the Comprehensive Test of Basic Skills, version 4 (CTBS-4). In a recent RAND report on a set of systemic reforms after just their first year, Klein et al. (2000) also found positive, though relatively small and sometimes insignificant, relationships between reform practices and student achievement in mathematics and science. The analysis at hand similarly investigates this question, but in the important context of a high-poverty district situated in a high-stakes accountability system.

Given the available data, we conducted two sets of analyses. First, for the entire district we examined the effects of student, teacher, and school characteristics on the fourth grade TAAS reading and mathematics scores. Data provided by the San Antonio district and other sources allowed for construction of a data set containing more than 3,800 fourth grade students in about 280 classrooms in all 64 elementary schools in the district. Individual TAAS reading and mathematics scores were regressed against student, teacher, classroom, and school characteristics using multilevel linear models to partition the variation in reading and mathematics achievement into student and classroom components. Second, we analyzed student achievement in a subsample of over 800 students in 63 classrooms for which teachers completed our survey.

The results at the district level provide the context for the subsample. Data gathered from the teacher surveys help inform the district analysis on the impacts of teacher practices and perceptions of student achievement. In addition, these students were administered the

Stanford-9 open-ended reading test, making possible an independent measure of student performance without the "high stakes" implications of the TAAS.

In the sections that follow, we discuss the operationalization of the variables included, identify the models estimated, describe the methods used, and analyze the results of those regressions.

DISTRICT-LEVEL DATA AND DEPENDENT VARIABLES

In each of the models presented, individual test scores are used to measure student achievement. The district-wide data set consists of all fourth grade students in San Antonio during the 1997–1998 school year who had valid scores on both the reading and mathematics sections of the TAAS.[2]

Because of the sweeping changes in the district during the 1998–1999 school year, we decided to limit the analysis to the 1997–1998 school year, even though data from the 1998–1999 school year were also available. During site visits and classroom observations in spring 1998, design implementation was clearly under way in many schools. By the same time in 1999, however, implementation of NAS designs had been pushed to the background. The district had mandated more uniform reforms. As described in the previous chapters, instruction in all classrooms was fairly generic and focused on preparation for the TAAS. Any effects from NAS implementation would be more likely found in the 1997–1998 data set.

At the district level, TLI scores from the reading and mathematics sections of the TAAS are the dependent variables in separate sets of

---

[2]The original data files provided by San Antonio contained records on 4,509 students. Of these, many did not have test scores because they were enrolled in alternative education centers or were exempt from the TAAS because of special education or limited English proficiency status. A smaller proportion of students were excluded from the sample because one or both of their scores were missing. Of these, some may have been absent when the TAAS was administered or had invalid results because of coding irregularities. On average, we found no statistically significant differences in characteristics between students who were not exempt from the TAAS, but did not have valid scores, and those included in the data set used for the models we analyze here.

regression models.[3] For ease of interpretation, these scores are standardized to have a mean of zero and a standard deviation of one.[4]

OPERATIONALIZING THE INDEPENDENT VARIABLES

Student Characteristics

Students in the San Antonio Independent School District (SAISD) come from fairly homogeneous backgrounds. Most are Latino, and from low-income families. Nevertheless, it is important to understand how differences between individual students, such as their socioeconomic characteristics, English language ability, mobility patterns, and prior achievement affect their performance as measured by standardized test scores.

In our models, we include dummy variables for each student's gender (male as reference), and race or ethnicity (African American or white or other[5] vs. Latino). Many students in Texas whose primary language is Spanish are exempt from the TAAS and instead take a version of the instrument in Spanish. Others, however, are not considered exempt, even though they are enrolled in bilingual education programs or classified as limited English proficient. We constructed dummy variables to account for bilingual or limited English proficient students in the data set.

Eligibility for free or reduced price lunch programs is used as a proxy for low income. San Antonio is a Title I district, so all students are

[3]These scores are transformations of raw estimates of student ability scaled to have a mean of 70 (reflecting the standard for passing) and a standard deviation of 15. Succinctly, "The TLI is not a percentage of items correct. It is a standard score. Its primary functions are to describe how far above or below the passing standard the student is and to indicate whether the student is making learning progress over time" (*Texas Student Assessment Program Technical Digest for the Academic Year 1999–2000*, p. 30; Texas Education Agency; http://www.tea.state.tx.us/student.assessment/resources/techdig/chap5.pdf).

[4]The TLI scores are significantly skewed to the right. To satisfy normality assumptions in our estimation methods, before standardizing the TLI scores we transformed each set of scores using the Box-Cox method (for details see Greene, 2000, p. 444).

[5]The number of Asian American/Pacific Islander and Native American students is very small in this sample and their test scores do not differ significantly from the scores of white students, so these four categories were combined into "white or other."

automatically enrolled in free lunch programs. The district, however, keeps track of family income and calculates which students would normally be eligible for these programs. A dummy variable was constructed using this information provided by the district. We also include dummy variables for students in special education and gifted and talented programs. Age is a continuous variable, calculated from each student's date of birth up to the last day of April 1998, the month when the TAAS was administered.

We include a measure of student mobility, calculated from dates of entry and withdrawal provided by the district and defined as the total number of weeks students spent in the classroom where the TAAS was administered.

As a proxy for prior student achievement, we include the 1997 TAAS reading or mathematics TLI scores corresponding to the dependent variable. These test scores from the previous school year are also standardized to have a mean of zero and standard deviation of one. For those students who did not have valid scores from 1997 we impute the mean value and create a missing score indicator dummy variable to control for this imputation.

Teacher Background and Classroom Characteristics

As discussed in Chapter One, understanding the relationship between student achievement and classroom environments is key to this analysis. Furthermore, the particular composition of students within classrooms may also be an important determinant of student ability and we examine the relationship between average classroom characteristics and achievement.

We include teacher background characteristics, such as gender, race or ethnicity, educational degree, and years of teaching experience. Operationalization of these measures is straightforward. Dummy variables were constructed for gender (female as reference), race or ethnicity (African American or white or other vs. Latino), and educational degree (master's vs. bachelor's). Also included are total years' teaching experience.

Measures designed to control for classroom effects were constructed by taking each of the individual student characteristics and calculating means for all the students linked to a particular teacher. The first set of variables at this level includes the proportion of students in each classroom who are male, African American or white or other; enrolled in a bilingual education program; classified as limited English proficient; eligible for free or reduced price lunch; and in special education or in gifted and talented programs. The other variables at the classroom level consist of means calculated for student age, number of weeks in the classroom, and the appropriate 1997 TAAS reading or mathematics score (with respect to the dependent variable).

School Characteristics

Within our two-level framework, the proportion of variance that can be directly attributable to differences between schools, rather than between classrooms, is not specifically calculated. It is still important, however, to take into account the effect of schoolwide characteristics on student performance. We include two such variables here. The first is a proxy for relative school quality. Each year the TEA issues Accountability Ratings, based primarily on TAAS passage rates and attendance rates.[6] We assigned each of the four possible ratings a number from one to four (i.e., 1 = Low performing, 2 = Acceptable, 3 = Recognized, 4 = Exemplary) and for each school in the district sample we calculated average TEA ratings from 1995–1997 (i.e., from the inception of the ratings to the year prior to our achievement data).

A second schoolwide variable captures differences between NAS and non-NAS schools. Since the impact of a NAS design on a given campus may develop over time, the variable is the number of years a school has been implementing the design. We give non-NAS schools a zero to allow the variable to function as a weighted dummy for NAS schools.[7]

---

[6]For more information, see http://www.tea.state.tx.us/perfreport/account/.

[7]Given the available data, it was also possible to estimate design-specific models. The results of these, however, did not enhance the present analysis and were not included here.

STUDENT ACHIEVEMENT IN SAN ANTONIO: MULTILEVEL ANALYSIS

Since students are nested within classrooms, we relied on multilevel modeling techniques to provide more accurate estimates of student- and classroom-level effects (see Bryk and Raudenbush, 1992; Bryk, Raudenbush, and Congdon, 1996; Singer, 1998).

The models separated the variance in the dependent variables into student- and classroom-level components. The student-level independent variables are centered on their classroom means (for further explanation of these models see Appendix A).

The district-wide data consist of all fourth graders who had valid scores on the English version of the TAAS in the 1997–1998 school year. Students who were absent on the days of test administration or had irregular scores were not included in the sample.

ANALYSIS OF THE DISTRICT SAMPLE

For reference, the means and standard deviations for the variables in both the TAAS reading and mathematics models are reported in Table 6.1.

Student Characteristics. Most fourth graders in SAISD, about 84 percent, are Latino. The next largest group is also minority, as 11 percent are African American. White students account for only about 5 percent of the district sample. Close to 90 percent of students are from low-income families and are eligible for free or reduced price lunch. Students who had valid scores on both TAAS exams, and were also either enrolled in a bilingual education program or classified as limited English proficient made up approximately 10 percent of the sample. Over 11 percent of the sample consists of special education students who were not exempt from taking the TAAS.

Of particular note is the high mobility rate for the district sample. We set the maximum number of weeks of instruction as the weeks prior to the TAAS administration in April at 38. The average student in the sample missed up to two weeks of classroom time due to transfers between teachers or schools. During the 1997–1998 school year,

Table 6.1

Descriptive Statistics of Variables in Multilevel District Sample Analysis

Variables	Mean	SD
Dependent Variables		
TAAS reading score, 1998	75.03	16.19
TAAS mathematics score, 1998	71.58	15.40
Independent Variables for Students (n = 3,820)		
Percent male	49.06	
Race or ethnicity		
Percent African American	10.89	
Percent Asian American/Pacific Islander	0.10	
Percent Latino	83.56	
Percent Native American	0.10	
Percent White	5.29	
Percent in bilingual education program	11.91	
Percent with limited English proficiency	5.18	
Percent free/reduced price lunch program eligible	88.53	
Percent in special education	11.18	
Percent in gifted and talented education	6.91	
Age (n = 3,819)	10.31	0.45
Weeks in classroom	35.98	7.30
1997 TAAS reading score (n = 3,195)	66.06	22.78
1997 TAAS mathematics score (n = 3,116)	69.56	16.83
Percent of students in NAS schools (n = 1,906)	49.90	
Percent in Co-NECT schools (n = 229)	5.99	
Percent in ELOB schools (n = 190)	4.97	
Percent in MRSH schools (n = 574)	15.03	
Percent in SFA/RW schools (n = 913)	23.90	
Independent Variables for Teachers and Classrooms (n = 279)		
Percent male	11.47	
Total years teaching	13.53	8.96
Teacher race or ethnicity		
Percent African American	13.62	
Percent Asian American/Pacific Islander	0.36	
Percent Latino	48.39	
Percent Native American	0.36	
Percent White	37.28	
Percent with master's degree	38.35	
Classroom percent male	49.15	0.19
Classroom race or ethnicity		
Percent African American	10.06	0.20
Percent White or other	4.93	0.10
Classroom percent bilingual education program	21.35	0.38
Classroom percent limited English proficiency	5.33	0.11
Classroom percent free/reduced price lunch program eligible	89.33	0.13
Classroom percent special education	14.91	0.22

Table 6.1 (continued)

Variables	Mean	SD
Classroom percent gifted and talented education	5.80	0.10
Average age	10.34	0.26
Classroom average weeks in class	36.12	2.44
Classroom average 1997 TAAS reading score	63.55	14.35
Classroom average 1997 TAAS mathematics score	68.89	8.58
Percent teaching in NAS schools (n = 138)	49.46	
Percent teaching in Co-NECT schools (n = 15)	5.38	
Percent teaching in ELOB schools (n = 13)	4.66	
Percent teaching in MRSH schools (n = 40)	14.34	
Percent teaching in SFA/RW schools (n = 70)	25.09	
Independent Variables for schools (n = 64)		
1995–1997 average TEA rating	2.00	0.21
Years implementing a NAS design (NAS schools only, n = 32)	1.47	0.67
Percent of schools implementing a NAS design (n = 32)	50.00	
Percent implementing Co-NECT design (n = 3)	4.69	
Percent implementing ELOB design (n = 3)	4.69	
Percent implementing MRSH design (n = 9)	14.06	
Percent implementing SFA/RW design (n = 17)	26.56	

almost half of students in the sample were in NAS schools, and almost half of these students were in SFA/RW.

Teacher Background and Classroom Characteristics. Less than 12 percent of fourth grade teachers in San Antonio are male, and most are either Latino (about 48 percent) or white (about 37 percent). The average teaching experience is almost 14 years, with a standard deviation of about nine years. A little over one-third (about 38 percent) of teachers in this larger district sample have earned master's degrees. The percentage of teachers in NAS schools and linked to specific designs is roughly proportional to the distribution of students between NAS and non-NAS schools and within specific designs.

Given the distribution of students, we did not have information on class size and could not attach any kind of weighting for class size within the model specification. The classroom means calculated for each of the student characteristics all roughly correspond to the individual student means.

School Characteristics. The mean of 2.0 for TEA ratings from 1995 to 1997 reflects the fact that almost all the schools in the sample had

Acceptable ratings during these years. On average, schools had been implementing NAS designs for one or two years prior to the 1998 TAAS administration.

MULTIVARIATE RESULTS FOR SAN ANTONIO

We estimated the model above for both the TAAS reading and mathematics scores to examine the relationships between student achievement and student and classroom characteristics. The estimation results are given in Table 6.2. Since the dependent variables have been standardized, a coefficient represents the increment change in the dependent variable from a unit increase in the independent variable.

STUDENT-LEVEL EFFECTS

In general, the socioeconomic factors examined (race or ethnicity and family income) were important predictors in the models. Students in the white/other category tended to perform better than Latinos by 0.15 of a standard deviation (SD) in reading and 0.11 of an SD in mathematics. Students who were eligible for free or reduced price lunch programs had significantly lower scores than students who were not eligible by 0.14 of an SD in reading and 0.09 of an SD in mathematics.

The variables related to language (bilingual and limited English proficient) were not statistically significant, implying that these students had mastered English to a level sufficient for them to be legitimately grouped with other students taking the TAAS that year.

Students who are grouped into either special education or talented and gifted categories had significantly different achievement-level scores from other students. Students in special education had significantly lower test scores than other students by nearly half of an SD. The implication here is that the average abilities of students in special education, who are not exempt from the TAAS, are not at the same level as other students taking the TAAS. In addition, students who are in talented and gifted programs scored 0.51 of an SD higher than other students in reading and 0.39 of an SD higher in mathematics.

Table 6.2

Multilevel Results for the Relationships of District-Wide 1998 Fourth Grade TAAS Scores to Student, Classroom, and School Factors

Variables	Reading		Mathematics	
	Coefficient	SE	Coefficient	SE
Intercept	0.31	1.34	2.75	1.48
Independent Variables for Students (n = 3,820)				
Male	−0.03	0.02	0.02	0.02
African American	−0.08	0.05	−0.01	0.04
White or other	0.15[a]	0.05	0.11[b]	0.05
Bilingual education program	0.00	0.08	−0.03	0.08
Limited English proficiency	0.05	0.06	0.00	0.06
Free/reduced price lunch program eligible	−0.14[a]	0.05	−0.09[b]	0.04
Special education	−0.47[a]	0.04	−0.51[a]	0.04
Gifted and talented education	0.51[a]	0.05	0.39[a]	0.05
Age	−0.09[a]	0.03	−0.10[a]	0.02
Weeks in classroom	0.01[a]	0.00	0.004[b]	0.002
1997 TAAS reading score	0.53[a]	0.01	__c	__c
1997 TAAS mathematics score	__c	__c	0.57[a]	0.01
Missing 1997 TAAS reading score	−0.11[a]	0.04	__c	__c
Missing 1997 TAAS mathematics score	__c	__c	−0.21[a]	0.04
Independent Variables for Classrooms and Teachers (n = 279)				
Male teacher	−0.02	0.06	−0.05	0.07
Years of teaching experience	−0.05	0.06	−0.04	0.07
African American teacher	−0.08	0.05	−0.05	0.05
White or other teacher	0.00	0.00	0.00	0.00
Master's degree	−0.02	0.04	−0.03	0.05
Classroom percent male	−0.31[b]	0.14	−0.16	0.15
Classroom percent African American	0.09	0.10	−0.09	0.12
Classroom percent White or other	0.61[b]	0.25	0.63[b]	0.29
Classroom percent bilingual education program	−0.11	0.08	−0.05	0.08
Classroom percent limited English proficiency	0.02	0.20	−0.18	0.23
Classroom percent free/reduced price lunch program eligible	−0.07	0.21	−0.07	0.25
Classroom percent special education	−0.41[b]	0.16	−0.76[a]	0.16
Classroom percent gifted and talented education	0.91[a]	0.21	0.80[a]	0.25
Classroom average age	−0.12	0.12	−0.34[b]	0.13
Classroom average weeks in classroom	0.01	0.01	0.01	0.01

Table 6.2 (continued)

Variables	Reading		Mathematics	
	Coefficient	SE	Coefficient	SE
Classroom average 1997 TAAS reading score	0.54[a]	0.06	__c	__c
Classroom average 1997 TAAS mathematics score	__c	__c	0.45[a]	0.06
Classroom percent missing 1997 TAAS reading score	−0.13	0.14	__c	__c
Classroom percent missing 1997 TAAS mathematics score	__c	__c	−0.18	0.15
Independent Variables for Schools (n = 64)				
Average Texas Education Agency rating, 1995–1997	0.35[a]	0.11	0.26[b]	0.13
Years implementing a NAS design	−0.03	0.02	−0.03	0.03

NOTE: SE is standard error.

[a]Significant at 0.01 level (highlighted in bold).

[b]Significant at 0.05 level (highlighted in bold).

[c]Excluded from the model.

The average number of weeks students spent in the classroom showed small but significant effects. This result may have been influenced by the choice of sample, since students taking both tests are likely less mobile. The extremely small coefficient in math may also reflect the fact that each school in the district was implementing an Everyday Mathematics program, which required every math teacher to be "on the same page at the same time." Thus, students were likely to face less discontinuity in mathematics instruction if they moved to other schools within the district.

The strongest predictor of fourth grade scores was the scores students achieved in third grade. If students scored higher in third grade, they were also likely to score higher in fourth grade, net of all other student, teacher, classroom, and school characteristics.

TEACHER- AND CLASSROOM-LEVEL EFFECTS

Overall, none of the variables measuring teacher characteristics in these models have significant effects on student performance at the second level of analysis.

Differences between classrooms in terms of their demographic makeup seem to matter along lines similar to corresponding student-level effects. One interesting exception is the effect of the class gender composition on reading scores. At the individual student level, we saw no difference in performance between boys and girls in fourth grade. At the classroom level, the results suggest that classes with more boys than girls tend to have lower average reading scores by about three-tenths of an SD.

In addition, classes with higher proportions of students in the white/other category tend to out-perform classes that are predominantly Latino. The proportion of students in the classroom who are either in special education or in gifted and talented education is also significant in both models. Classrooms with a higher proportion of students who are older than average tend to have lower math scores.

SCHOOL-LEVEL EFFECTS

Average TEA rating is significant (0.35 of an SD in reading and 0.26 in mathematics), suggesting that relative school quality is an important factor in student achievement. Implicit is a confirmation that the rating system employed by TEA has indeed identified those schools in which student performance on average has not improved over time.[8]

After controlling for all of these student, classroom, and school characteristics, we fail to find a significant effect of implementation of NAS designs in San Antonio. This same result came up in estimations of a variety of other model specifications, using other regression techniques such as ordinary least squares, three-level linear models, and probit models, where the dependent variables were binary indicators of passing or failing scores.

This is not surprising since we are examining effects on spring 1998 scores and many of the designs had not been in place that long. However, note that the focus here is establishing a baseline in the

---

[8]The TEA ratings for the three school years 1994–1995 through 1996–1997 are based, in part, on passing rates for students on the state assessments. We did not include the 1997–1998 school year TEA ratings to avoid confounding of spring 1997–1998 school TEA ratings and an individual student's test scores in the spring of 1998.

district to set the stage for the subsequent analyses of classroom conditions in the RAND sample. We analyze the 1997–1998 school year data because this is the time when instructional effects are likely to occur given the changes that we described in the districts between the 1997–1998 and 1998–1999 school years.

GOODNESS OF FIT

To establish a baseline for a simple measure of goodness of fit, we partitioned the variance in student test scores into their within- and between-classroom components. Prior to estimating the full reading and mathematics models, a two-level ANOVA regression was used to estimate within- and between-classroom variance in the district for both TAAS reading and mathematics scores. The results are given in Table 6.3, indicating in both cases that about 17 percent of the total variance in student achievement lies between classrooms and about 83 percent of variance within classrooms.

The results from the full district-level models in the same table show that the estimates explained at least half of the variance within classrooms. While the reading model estimates explain more than two-thirds of the variation in test scores between classrooms, a substantial portion of between-classroom variation remains unexplained. Results for the mathematics model estimates are even lower as only about 45 percent of the variance between classrooms is explained.

Table 6.3

Variance in Student Test Scores Explained by District Sample Models

	Reading	Mathematics
ANOVA		
Variance within classrooms	0.839	0.839
Variance between classrooms	0.169	0.165
District Models		
Variance within classrooms	0.446	0.422
Variance between classrooms	0.056	0.092
Percent of variance within classrooms explained by the model	46.85	49.74
Percent of variance between classrooms explained by the model	66.96	44.47

These findings concur with similar analyses of student scores in the context of classrooms and schools (see Lee et al., 1998; Gamoran, 1992; Lee and Bryk, 1989). The results have important implications for educators and policymakers, especially within a context of high-stakes accountability and implementation of NAS designs. If most of the differences in student outcomes come from within classrooms and are student specific, rather than between classrooms, then school reform efforts which focus on instructional practices might not be able to produce desired results.

To examine the impact of teaching practices and classroom environments in the next section we attempt to further control for variation at the classroom level by incorporating data collected from the teacher survey into the analysis.

RAND'S SURVEY SAMPLE DATA AND DEPENDENT VARIABLES

To learn more about the effects of the classroom environment and teaching practices on student achievement, we now extend the models previously discussed to include data from the teacher survey and the Stanford-9. The data set used here was constructed by taking a convenience sample of fourth grade students in the 1998–1999 school year who, in addition to valid TAAS reading and mathematics scores, had valid scores on the RAND administration of the Stanford-9, and were in classrooms where their teachers completed the 1998 survey.

In addition to regressions on TAAS reading and writing scores, a third model takes the Stanford-9 results, reported as Normal Curve Equivalent (NCE) scores as the dependent variable.[9] Again, for ease of interpretation, all the scores are standardized to have a mean of zero and a standard deviation of one.[10]

---

[9]Stanford-9 reading NCE scores represent a student's position in a normal distribution of Stanford-9 raw scores nationwide. The NCE scores are scaled to have a mean of 50 and a standard deviation of 21.06 and do not correspond precisely to percentile rankings.

[10]No further transformations were required for the Stanford-9 scores as the distribution fit normality assumptions required for our regression techniques.

Classroom-level variables, such as the percent male or in special education, from the district sample were used in this analysis, since the classroom environments would not change for students in a sub-sample.

ADDITIONAL INDEPENDENT VARIABLES FROM THE TEACHER SURVEY

Independent variables constructed from survey responses include three individual items and four of the teacher indices discussed in Chapters Four and Five. One additional composite of related survey items was created for inclusion in the quantitative analysis.

Key to our analysis is the inclusion of variables related to instructional conditions in classrooms. To examine the effects on student performance of the extent to which teachers employ specific strategies we construct variables reflecting traditional and more reform-like practices.

The first three variables added to the model are items from the teacher survey viewed as measures of traditional instructional strategies:

- Lecture,
- Students work individually on written assignments/worksheets in class, and
- Students practice or drill on computational skills that we would expect to be used less frequently within the context of educational reform.

These are from a section of the survey that asked teachers how often specific instructional strategies were used in the classroom. Responses were ranked on a 5-point scale with 1 = never, 2 = once or twice a semester, 3 = once or twice a month, 4 = once or twice a week, and 5 = almost every day.

The reform composite, described in Chapter Five, is added as a measure of reform-like instructional strategies. It is a continuous variable consisting of responses from 15 items, standardized to have a mean of zero and a standard deviation of one across two scales (the

5-point scale mentioned above and a 4-point scale that ranges from 1 = almost never to 4 = every lesson). The alpha reliability of this composite was 0.77 for both 1998 and 1999.

Other variables are constructed from indices designed to measure teachers' perceptions of their students' ability and readiness to learn, and general factors in the school climate including:

- *Factors hindering student achievement:* Teachers were asked to rank the extent to which a number of factors might hinder their students from achieving at high levels in schools. These include lack of basic skills, inadequate prior student preparation in the subject area, lack of student motivation, inadequate support from parents for students, and lack of student discipline. Each was ranked on a 4-point scale with 1 = greatly and 4 = not at all. We combined teacher responses on these items into an additive composite of factors hindering student achievement; the alpha reliability for this composite was 0.79, and the correlations ranged from 0.26 to 0.35.

- *Collaboration:* A continuous variable consisting of teacher responses to six items, standardized to have a mean of zero and a standard deviation of one across two scales (6 points ranging from 1 = does not describe my school to 6 = clearly describes my school and 4 points ranging from 1 = strongly disagree to 4 = strongly agree) (for more details see Chapter Four).

- *Principal leadership:* A continuous variable consisting of teacher responses to seven items on a 4-point scale ranging from 1 = strongly disagree to 4 = strongly agree (for more details see Chapter Four).

- *Quality of professional development:* A continuous variable consisting of teacher responses to ten items on a 4-point scale ranging from 1 = strongly disagree to 4 = strongly agree (for more details see Chapter Four).

MULTILEVEL ANALYSIS IN THE SURVEY SAMPLE

To learn more about the effects of the classroom environment and teaching practices on achievement scores, we extend the model used to analyze student achievement in the district by including the eight classroom-level measures. In addition to modeling the TAAS scores as before, we also analyze Stanford-9 scores for the sample using the same model used to investigate the effects of student and classroom characteristics. Thus, we are able to examine whether the instructional conditions consistent with what NAS designs are intended to promote in schools are related to student achievement on a high-stakes test (e.g., TAAS reading) as well as an independent commercial assessment with no stakes attached (Stanford-9). The model specification is described in Appendix A.

ANALYSIS OF THE SURVEY SAMPLE

Table 6.4 gives the means and standard deviations for all variables included in the Stanford-9 and the TAAS reading and mathematics models of the survey sample. Difference of means tests revealed no statistically significant differences in student or teacher characteristics between the district and the survey samples. Since classroom averages linked to students in the survey sample have not changed, they are not presented here. Compared with the district as a whole, the survey sample had slightly higher percentages of students and teachers in NAS schools (approximately 60 percent and 64 percent compared to 50 percent and 49 percent, respectively), given the nature of initial decisions as to which schools were selected to participate in the teacher survey (compare Table 6.4 with Table 6.1).

MULTILEVEL RESULTS FOR THE SURVEY SAMPLE

To focus on the new information gained from extending the model, we report only coefficient estimates for the teacher survey variables (Table 6.5). The estimation results for the rest of the variables in the models revealed few changes in comparison to the district models. In particular, the variables relating implementation of NAS designs to student outcomes in the survey sample were not significant.

The coefficient estimates summarized in Table 6.5 indicate that principal leadership does have an important effect on student achievement. The coefficients are significant for the state-mandated TAAS reading and mathematics tests, and while not significant, only slightly smaller for the Stanford-9 reading test. Previous studies

Table 6.4

Descriptive Statistics of 1998 Sample Data

Variables	Mean	SD
Dependent Variables		
Stanford-9 reading score	43.03	21.55
TAAS reading score, 1998	76.54	15.88
TAAS mathematics score, 1998	73.15	15.21
Independent Variables for Students (n = 861)		
Percent male	45.53	
Race or ethnicity		
Percent African American	10.92	
Percent Asian/Pacific Islander	0.12	
Percent Hispanic	79.91	
Percent Native American	0.23	
Percent White	8.71	
Percent free/reduced price lunch program eligible	88.85	
Percent in special education	10.10	
Percent in gifted and talented education	7.78	
Percent in bilingual education program	7.08	
Percent with limited English proficiency	7.08	
1997 TAAS reading score (n = 730)	69.45	22.08
1997 TAAS mathematics score (n = 713)	72.54	15.29
Age on test date (4/30/1998)	10.30	0.44
Number of weeks in classroom	36.31	6.63
Percent of students in NAS schools (n = 516)	59.93	
Percent in Co-NECT schools (n = 71)	8.25	
Percent in ELOB schools (n = 30)	3.48	
Percent in MRSH schools (n = 133)	15.45	
Percent in SFA/RW schools (n = 282)	32.75	
Teacher Characteristics (n = 63)		
Percent male	7.94	
Total years teaching	13.11	8.71
Teacher race or ethnicity		
Percent African American	12.70	
Percent Asian/Pacific Islander	0.00	
Percent Hispanic	49.21	
Percent Native American	0.00	
Percent White	38.10	
Percent with master's degree	44.44	
Percent teaching in NAS schools (n = 40)	63.49	
Percent teaching in Co-NECT schools (n = 6)	9.52	
Percent teaching in ELOB schools (n = 2)	3.17	
Percent teaching in MRSH schools (n = 10)	15.87	
Percent teaching in SFA/RW schools (n = 22)	34.92	

Table 6.4 (continued)

Variables	Mean	SD
Responses to Teacher Survey Questions		
How often did you use each of the following instructional strategies with your class last year? (1 = never, 5 = almost every day)		
Lecture (n = 62)	4.44	0.92
Have students work individually on written assignments/ worksheets in class (n = 62)	4.58	0.56
Have students practice or drill computational skills (n = 63)	4.40	0.66
Teacher Survey Composites		
Collaboration[a]	0.00	1.00
Factors hindering student achievement (1 = greatly worsened, 5 = greatly improved)	1.82	0.63
Principal leadership composite (1 = strongly disagree, 4 = strongly agree)	2.32	0.69
Quality of professional development composite (1 = strongly disagree, 4 = strongly agree)	2.82	0.63
Reform composite[a]	0.00	1.00
School Characteristics (n = 23)		
1995–1997 average Texas Education Agency rating	2.06	0.26
Years implementing a NAS design (NAS schools only, n = 15)	1.27	0.46
Percent of schools implementing a NAS design (n = 15)	65.22	
Percent implementing Co-NECT design (n = 2)	8.70	
Percent implementing ELOB design (n = 1)	4.35	
Percent implementing MRSH design (n = 4)	17.39	
Percent implementing SFA/RW design (n = 8)	34.78	

[a]Constructed with mean 0, standard deviation 1 to homogenize the various response formats in the items that constitute the composite.

(Berends and Kirby et al., 2001; Kirby et al., 2001) found teacher perceptions of principal leadership to be an important component in NAS design implementation. These results suggest that principal leadership as measured by this set of survey items also has a significant effect on achievement in general.

But whether looking at state-mandated exams or the independent Stanford-9, the extended models find little support for effects of either reform-like or traditional instructional strategies alike, net of other student- and classroom-level factors. The exception is the significantly positive effect on TAAS mathematics scores generated by having students complete assignments or worksheets in class. This finding could possibly be a consequence of the district-mandated Everyday Mathematics program, which tends to

Table 6.5

Multilevel Results for the Relationships Between Classroom Conditions and 1998 Fourth Grade Test Scores

	Stanford-9 Reading		TAAS Reading		TAAS Mathematics	
	Coefficient	SE	Coefficient	SE	Coefficient	SE
Instructional Strategies						
Lecture	−0.03	0.05	0.03	0.04	0.00	0.04
Students work individually on written assignment/worksheets in class	0.08	0.09	0.07	0.08	**0.15**[a]	0.07
Students practice or drill on computational skills	0.14	0.08	0.07	0.06	0.12	0.06
Teacher Survey Composites						
Collaboration	−0.02	0.08	0.11	0.06	0.09	0.06
Factors hindering student achievement	−0.03	0.07	−0.08	0.06	**−0.15**[a]	0.06
Principal leadership	0.12	0.09	**0.15**[a]	0.07	**0.21**[a]	0.07
Quality of professional development	0.12	0.09	0.05	0.07	−0.02	0.07
Reform	0.11	0.11	0.03	0.09	0.13	0.09

NOTE: SE is standard error.

[a]Significant at 0.01 level (highlighted in bold).

emphasize the use of worksheets in workbooks, and/or because of test preparation for the TAAS.

SUMMARY

This chapter deepens our understanding of the impact of NAS designs and classroom practices within a context of high poverty and high-stakes accountability through quantitative analysis of student achievement at the high point of a NAS implementation. As expected because of the early stages of implementation, NAS designs had no significant effects on student achievement, as measured by TAAS reading and mathematics scores. However, this does contrast what others found early on in the implementation process in other settings (see Ross et al., 2001).

To further inform this result, we examined test scores for a subsample of students who were linked to teachers in our survey data. Using survey data to control further for classroom practices and teacher perceptions of classroom environments, we still found no statistically significant effect from implementation of NAS designs.

More important, we did not find that instructional conditions promoted by reforms such as NAS—including teacher-reported collaboration, quality of professional development, and reform-like instructional practices—were related to student achievement net of other student and classroom conditions.

There may be several explanations for these findings. First, the instructional analyses were based on a small sample size of 63 classrooms, and this small sample may not have been powerful enough to detect classroom-level effects of reform-like practices (most of the effects of reform-like practices in Table 6.5 were positive in sign but statistically insignificant). Second, the levels for these reform-like practices were not at extremely high levels to truly test whether such variation was related to student achievement. We attempted to provide the most likely case for such effects to occur by analyzing 1997–1998 data when instructional conditions tended to differ. By the following year, most classrooms were more similar in their instruction, which was more conventional in nature. Third, a related reason is that because of the pressure of the district to improve TAAS achievement scores and the constraints on teacher practice of curricular mandates, teachers may have reported on surveys that they spent time on certain reform-like activities, but such reports in reality may have been much less reform-like. Fourth, it may be that the teacher-reported measures here were not well aligned with the outcomes examined, which is critical when examining instructional effects on achievement (Cohen and Hill, 2000; Gamoran et al., 1997, 1995; Newmann & Associates, 1996). Studies of instruction have not found robust effects of pedagogical practices on student achievement across scores (see Mayer, 1999; Gamoran et al., 1995; Burstein et al., 1995). Certainly, this is an issue that deserves further research, particularly in schools and classrooms in which whole-school designs have been fully implemented and sustained over a longer period of time.

Chapter Seven

IMPLICATIONS FOR SCHOOL IMPROVEMENT IN
HIGH-POVERTY SETTINGS

Rather than reiterate the summary of findings that occur within each chapter, we focus here on the implications of school improvement efforts such as NAS in high-poverty settings.

Currently, many schools throughout the country are attempting NAS-like reforms using the federal funding provided by such programs as Title I and the CSRD program. Our study in conjunction with the other RAND studies on NAS has clear implications. Schools attempting comprehensive school reforms face many obstacles during implementation, and because of this, whole-school designs face continuing challenges in significantly raising the achievement of all students. This is important to remember when setting expectations for school improvement under new federal, state, and local programs—particularly when implementing strategies and interventions in high-poverty, low-performing settings.

Because the target of the federal Title I and CSRD funds is primarily high-poverty schools, schools most likely to be affected by the CSRD program are also schools that are most likely to face very fragmented and conflicting environments, difficult and changing political currents, new accountability systems, entrenched unions, serious lack of resources in terms of teacher time, and demoralized teachers given the fluctuating reform agenda, and the difficult task of improving student performance under these types of conditions (for a description of CSRD schools see Kirby et al., in review).

Given this, federal and state policymakers need to think critically about their current stance of simultaneously promoting: high-stakes testing; the implementation of comprehensive school reforms that promote innovative curriculum and instructional strategies; and the implementation of multiple concurrent reforms. The implementation of high-stakes testing regimes—the apparent outcome of many standards-based reforms—might preclude the adoption of rich and varied curricula that challenge students and motivate them toward more in-depth learning experiences. It certainly prevents adoption of such curricula when other reforms emphasizing only basic skills instruction are mandated on top of the design-based curriculum. The current study shows that high-stakes tests are a two-edged sword in this environment. On the one hand, high-stakes tests motivate schools to increase performance and often to seek out new curriculum and instructional strategies associated with comprehensive school reforms. On the other hand, those very same tests provide disincentives to adopt richer, more in-depth curriculum.

TOWARD BETTER EDUCATIONAL POLICY

Our findings are consistent with Porter and Clune's scheme for better educational policy (Porter et al., 1988; Porter, 1994; Clune, 1998). They posit that educational policies such as comprehensive school reform are likely to influence teachers and students to the extent to which they are specific, powerful, authoritative, consistent, and stable. *Specificity*, or depth, is the extent to which the comprehensive school reform provides detailed guidance or materials to help schools and teachers understand what they are supposed to do (e.g., materials that describe the stages of implementing the design and ongoing, clear assistance strategies to further promote implementation). *Power* refers to the rewards or sanctions attached to the whole-school reform, such as teachers receiving bonuses or greater autonomy if they comply with implementing the design. *Authority* refers to the degree to which the reform policy is seen as *legitimate* and as having the *support* of those who are responsible for implementation. If respected groups or policymakers have strong positive views toward whole-school reform and if teachers support its implementation, the design is likely to have greater influence in changing teaching and learning. *Consistency* or *alignment* refers to the extent to which the set of whole-school interventions and strategies are aligned with a common mission and vision, both within the school and the district. *Stability* refers to the reform being sustained over time in a coherent, consistent manner. Policymakers and educators should use these dimensions as a means for thinking critically about the comprehensive school reform being considered and whether the conditions exist for it to flourish.

Specificity

In the case of San Antonio, the specificity of the designs varied as did the detailed guidance provided by the district and design teams. The district was supportive of the designs and promoted their adoption throughout the district. In addition, the district devoted a great deal of financial resources and professional development to schools and teachers to change the learning environments for San Antonio students. Yet, over time, the specificity of the mathematics and reading initiatives far outweighed the specificity of the designs. As shown by interviews and observations, for example, elementary school teachers were expected to be within a certain page of the Everyday Mathematics workbooks, and district staff conducted checks in schools to ensure this was happening. Because of the structure of these other initiatives and the time that such prescriptiveness took, there was little time left over for design team activities, no matter how specific those may have been.

Moreover, about a third of the NAS teachers in our longitudinal teacher sample reported that the lack of coherent, sustained professional development hindered their students' success. About 15 percent of non-NAS teachers reported such a hindrance. This contrast suggests that the specificity of the district's professional development strategies for the mix of reforms was overwhelming to NAS teachers, who were implementing the entire set of reforms in the district.

Even the design teams themselves differ in the level of specificity that they provide schools. On the one hand, SFA/RW provides specific training and materials to schools to structure the reading program for elementary-level students. In addition, assessments are provided to ensure that grouping arrangements remain flexible and students can move every six to eight weeks or every grading period to a new group, if necessary, that meets their educational needs. On the other hand, ELOB offers little specific curricular guidance, providing teachers with learning principles and an emphasis on project-based learning. It is up to the teachers to develop the curriculum for the learning expeditions and all the units that comprise them.

As we found across all the designs, teacher training declined over time, and the design team representatives had less contact with schools and teachers over the course of this study. However, teachers desired more design team training to better understand the components and activities of the designs. They reported the need for more concrete, hands-on training that would enable them to better understand design processes and activities.

Power

There were very few rewards and sanctions associated with the NAS designs in San Antonio. While the superintendent had desired to have NAS designs be the integrative force to hold the district's reform efforts together, there were few rewards or sanctions for schools and teachers to adopt and implement the NAS reform. The stronger rewards and sanctions were associated with the TAAS, not with implementation of the designs. NAS designs were merely a weak tool that the district employed to bring about school change. As was clearly evident by the 1998–1999 school year, the district had invested more energy in its mathematics, reading, and language arts initiatives. Certainly, it was these that had more power for schools and teachers, not the NAS designs.

Thus, if districts and schools want to have whole-school reforms take hold in schools and be sustained over time, they will need to attend to the rewards, sanctions, and incentives associated with the reform. More important, they will need to attend to the rewards and sanctions linked to other reforms and assessments to understand whether implementation of whole-school reforms is in conflict or supported by the power of other reforms.

Authority

During the time of this study, NAS and its designs were all seeking greater authority. At the time of this study, only the SFA program had been noted as significantly improving students' test scores (see Herman et al., 1999). While there was some achievement evidence coming out of Memphis (see Ross et al., 2001), this work had not yet been published in a peer-reviewed journal and was specific to one jurisdiction.

As our interviews with teachers and district staff revealed, the district had hoped that NAS and its designs would be the glue to hold the district together. However, there were doubts about whether the designs could raise students' TAAS scores to the extent necessary to meet the state accountability requirements. Hedging its bets, the district added specific curricular programs to the mix of reforms, which in the end, pushed the NAS designs to the periphery of the everyday lives of students and teachers in classrooms.

To some degree, the lack of authority associated with the NAS reform in San Antonio may have led to a lack of teacher support for the designs. We found that teacher support for the designs declined from 54 percent in 1998 to 25 percent in 1999. In interviews, teachers expressed that they doubted whether the NAS designs alone helped their students build an academic foundation, which so many of them were lacking.

Over time, as some designs establish more of an evidentiary base for their practices and approaches, such authority will appeal to schools and districts. If designs and districts can integrate professional development and training over time, it is likely that ongoing support of teachers can be sustained rather than wane.

Coherence and Alignment

The policy of the NAS reform was not well aligned with the district-mandated initiatives. The district, schools, and teachers were aware of this—a pressing question with which all were struggling. In fact, during the time of our study, the district was pursuing how the NAS designs could be integrated with the mathematics, reading, and language arts frameworks it had put forth. This was certainly a difficult issue within the high-stakes environment.

Yet, while the district and teachers were living with this question, life in classrooms reflected that by the spring of 1999, fourth grade students spent half of their day on a very specific mathematics program and tightly structured reading and language arts frameworks. Clearly, district-issued curriculum and instructional strategies limited the ability of teachers to develop units, plan expeditions and lessons, and engage in instructional practices described in the NAS and design team literature. It was the district and state initiatives that directed the educational mission of all schools in San Antonio, not the NAS designs.

Further integration and forethought on behalf of districts and schools to integrate their reform strategies and interventions is a challenge in many environments, particularly high-poverty, low-performing ones. Yet, it is critical to align the reform policies, strategies, interventions, and supports for meaningful school improvement that continues over time.

Stability

After the data collection efforts for this study ended in the spring of 1999, a critical moment occurred—the superintendent's departure—followed by the decline of the NAS initiative in San Antonio.[1] As so often happens in urban school districts, the superintendent's position was tenuous with the school board. After a school board election in May, 1999, two new board members were elected—thus tipping the balance of the school board against her. Soon after, the superintendent accepted a generous buyout and resigned. Her resignation was accepted by a 4-3 vote by the school board. Her success in improving the test scores in San Antonio schools relative to the state, even though still lagging far behind, assured her a position elsewhere. She moved on.

The stability of the NAS designs in San Antonio was deeply affected by the superintendent's departure. During the summer of 1999, teachers were asked to vote whether or not to keep the designs. Whereas some schools initially adopted designs based on 60 percent of their teachers voting in favor of adoption, the summer 1999 vote required 80 percent of the teachers to vote in favor of keeping the

---

[1]This information is based on interviews with district staff and some design teams after the superintendent's departure as well as reports in the *San Antonio Express-News.*

design. The lack of support that existed in NAS schools, the overburdening that NAS teachers reported, and the uncertainty and tension within the district likely led to the substantial number of schools that voted to drop the designs.

The stability of the whole-school improvement efforts with NAS designs thus was on very fragile ground, even in a district that was initially so supportive of NAS implementation. Unfortunately, such instability is all too common in high-poverty settings. To put the policy pieces having the qualities mentioned here in place for reform, and to sustain them over time despite the changes in leadership, remains a significant challenge.

SCHOOL LEADERSHIP

In addition to the importance of district leadership in implementing policies that are specific, powerful, authoritative, aligned, and stable, the leadership in schools is also critical.

Despite all that was going on in the district and the overall similarity of instructional conditions, our analysis showed that principal leadership had a strong effect on student achievement scores. Controlling for other student, teacher, classroom, and school factors, classrooms in which teachers reported greater principal leadership had higher TAAS reading and mathematics scores by 0.15 and 0.21 of a standard deviation, respectively. Principal leadership in our analysis was measured by teacher reports about principals who clearly communicated what was expected of teachers, were supportive and encouraging of staff, obtained resources for the school, enforced rules for student conduct, talked with teachers regarding instructional practices, had confidence in the expertise of the teachers, and took a personal interest in the professional development of teachers.

Our previous analyses have shown the importance of principal leadership in implementing the designs (Berends and Kirby et al., 2001; Kirby et al., 2001), so the link between implementation and performance is likely to be important as more and more schools adopt comprehensive school reform. Therefore, the importance of principal leadership should not be overlooked when adopting and implementing whole-school reforms.

SUPPORT FOR SCHOOLWIDE REFORM

Our analyses show that the design teams had a difficult time in San Antonio because of the high-stakes accountability environment, the pressing need to improve test scores, and the lack of the qualities— depth/specificity, power, authority, consistency/alignment, and stability—of the policies directly related to design implementation.

We have argued that the implementation of designs in classrooms was affected by factors related to district, schools, teachers, and design teams. The findings here are consistent with what RAND has found in its other studies of NAS (Kirby et al., 2001; Bodilly, 1998; 2001; Berends and Kirby et al., 2001; Berends, 2000; Bodilly and Berends, 1999). Comprehensive reforms face many obstacles during implementation, and because of this, whole-school designs face continuing challenges in significantly raising the achievement of all students, particularly those in high-poverty settings. The key seems to be implementing the reform in such a way that it aligns with the other school reform efforts to ensure consistent implementation over time. The challenge for such improvement efforts to become schoolwide looms large in the current environment where leadership in high-poverty districts and schools is fragile and unstable, fraught with conflicting policies and reform efforts.

As policymakers and practitioners, we must continue to grapple with the questions: How can the designs become schoolwide? How can we shape policies related to comprehensive school reform to lead to meaningful school improvement efforts? What supports—of states, districts, design teams, and schools—are necessary for implementation to take hold and be sustained over time? We have attempted to shed some light on those critical aspects of policies that policymakers and practitioners can address when embarking on whole-school reform efforts.

Time will tell whether districts, schools, design teams, teachers, and NAS can make the appropriate adjustments in the implementing sites. Additional and more specific longitudinal achievement data over time will help assess the conditions under which design-based assistance can contribute to improving student performance. However, as this study has emphasized, it is critical to understand the local conditions in which whole-school reforms operate. Researchers need to understand the district reform policies and how principals and teachers within schools enact these reforms. Moreover, when comparing those schools that are implementing reforms with schools that are not (the "control" schools), understanding what actually is being implemented in the comparison schools sheds important light on our understanding of the entire reform effort. In high-poverty settings, then, it is as important to understand reform efforts in the "control" schools as it is in the "treatment" schools to provide a more comprehensive assessment.

Continued research is critical, then, for understanding what it takes to sustain reform efforts such as NAS and other comprehensive school reforms. If teachers, principals, designs, and districts can sustain their focus on the NAS designs to structure the educational policies and their enactment in schools and classrooms, it is likely that the designs will become not only more widespread across schools, but also deeper in their implementation within schools. Perhaps, they may even be sustained over a longer period of time. However, accomplishing that goal will involve better policy, more perseverance, and leadership at all levels.

MULTILEVEL MODELS USED TO EXAMINE RELATIONSHIPS AMONG CLASSROOM CONDITIONS AND STUDENT ACHIEVEMENT

Since students are nested within classrooms, we relied on multilevel modeling techniques to provide more accurate estimates of student and classroom-level effects (see Bryk and Raudenbush, 1992; Bryk, Raudenbush, and Congdon, 1996; Singer, 1998). We estimated a series of models both for all the students in the district and for the survey sample. Specific model specifications for these are described in turn.

ACHIEVEMENT MODELS FOR ALL STUDENTS IN THE DISTRICT

Using district-wide data, the models estimated for both reading and mathematics scores are specified as follows:

Individual Student Model (Level 1)

$Y_{ij} = \beta_{0j} + \beta_1(\text{Male}) + \beta_2(\text{African American}) + \beta_3(\text{White or Other}) + \beta_4(\text{Bilingual Education Program}) + \beta_5(\text{Limited English Proficiency}) + \beta_6(\text{Free/Reduced Price Lunch Program Eligible}) + \beta_7(\text{Special Education}) + \beta_8(\text{Gifted and Talented Education}) + \beta_9(\text{Age}) + \beta_{10}(\text{Weeks with Class}) + \beta_{11}(1997 \text{ TAAS Score}) + \beta_{12}(\text{Missing } 1997 \text{ TAAS Score}) + r_{ij},$

where

- Y_{ij} is the dependent variable, i.e., the TAAS reading or mathematics score for student i in classroom j;

- β_{0j} is the Level 1 constant term and the average value of the dependent variable in classroom j;

- β_{1-12} are the Level 1 coefficients for the listed independent variables; and

- r_{ij} is the Level 1 random effect.

Classroom Context Model (Level 2)

$\beta_{0j} = \gamma_0 + \gamma_1(\text{Male Teacher}) + \gamma_2(\text{African American Teacher}) + \gamma_3(\text{White or Other Teacher}) + \gamma_4(\text{Teacher's Years of Experience}) + \gamma_5(\text{Master's Degree or Higher}) + \gamma_6(\text{Male.}_j) + \gamma_7(\text{African American.}_j) + \gamma_8(\text{White or Other.}_j) + \gamma_9(\text{Bilingual Education Program.}_j) + \gamma_{10}(\text{Limited English Proficiency.}_j) + \gamma_{11}(\text{Free/Reduced Price Lunch Program Eligible.}_j) + \gamma_{12}(\text{Special Education.}_j) + \gamma_{13}(\text{Gifted and Talented Education.}_j) + \gamma_{14}(\text{Age.}_j) + \gamma_{15}(\text{Weeks with Class.}_j) + \gamma_{16}(\text{1997 TAAS Score.}_j) + \gamma_{17}(\text{Missing 1997 TAAS Score.}_j) + \gamma_{18}(\text{Average TEA Rating, 1995 to 1997}) + \gamma_{19}(\text{Years Implementing a NAS Design}) + u$,

where

- β_{0j} in this model is from the student-level equation above, and it is the average test score in classroom j;

- γ_0 is the constant term;

- γ_{1-19} are the Level 2 coefficients for the listed independent variables (any variable with a ".j" ending is the classroom average of students for that variable); and

- u is a Level 2 random effect.

ACHIEVEMENT MODELS FOR RAND SURVEY SAMPLE

Individual Student Model (Level 1)

At the student level, we use the same model specification as in the district-wide analysis for each of the TAAS reading, mathematics, and Stanford-9 regressions. Within the Stanford-9 model the 1997 TAAS readings scores are used to control for prior student achievement.

$Y_{ij} = \beta_{0j} + \beta_1$ (Male) $+ \beta_2$(African American) $+ \beta_3$(White or Other) $+$
$\quad \beta_4$(Bilingual Education Program) $+ \beta_5$(Limited English
$\quad$ Proficiency) $+ \beta_6$(Free/Reduced Price Lunch Program Eligible) $+$
$\quad \beta_7$(Special Education) $+ \beta_8$(Gifted and Talented Education) $+$
$\quad \beta_9$(Age) $+ \beta_{10}$(Weeks with Class) $+ \beta_{11}$(1997 TAAS Score) $+$
$\quad \beta_{12}$(Missing 1997 TAAS Score) $+ r_{ij}$,

where

- Y_{ij} is the dependent variable, i.e., the TAAS reading or mathematics score or the Stanford-9 score for student i in classroom j;

- β_{0j} is the Level 1 constant term and the average value of the dependent variable in classroom j;

- β_{1-12} are the Level 1 coefficients for the listed independent variables;

- r_{ij} is the Level 1 random effect.

Classroom Context Model (Level 2)

$\beta_{0j} = \gamma_0 + \gamma_1$(Male Teacher) $+ \gamma_2$(African American Teacher) $+ \gamma_3$(White or Other Teacher) $+ \gamma_4$(Teacher's Years of Experience) $+$
$\quad \gamma_5$(Master's Degree or Higher)$+ \gamma_6$(Male.$_j$) $+ \gamma_7$(African American.$_j$) $+ \gamma_8$(White or Other.$_j$) $+ \gamma_9$(Bilingual Education Program.$_j$) $+ \gamma_{10}$(Limited English Proficiency.$_j$) $+$
$\quad \gamma_{11}$(Free/Reduced Price Lunch Program Eligible.$_j$) $+ \gamma_{12}$(Special Education.$_j$) $+ \gamma_{13}$(Gifted and Talented Education.$_j$) $+ \gamma_{14}$(Age.$_j$) $+$
$\quad \gamma_{15}$(Weeks with Class.$_j$) $+ \gamma_{16}$(1997 TAAS Score.$_j$) $+ \gamma_{17}$(Missing 1997 TAAS Score.$_j$) $+ \gamma_{18}$(Average TEA Rating, 1995 to 1997) $+$
$\quad \gamma_{19}$(Years Implementing a NAS Design) $+ \gamma_{20}$(Lecture) $+$
$\quad \gamma_{21}$(Worksheets) $+ \gamma_{22}$(Drill on Computational Skills) $+$
$\quad \gamma_{23}$(Collaboration) $+ \gamma_{24}$(Factors Hindering Student

Achievement) + γ_{25}(Principal Leadership) + γ_{26}(Quality of Professional Development) + γ_{27} (Reform) + u,

where

* β_{0j} in this model is from the student-level equation above, and it is the average test score in classroom j;

* γ_0 is the intercept term;

* γ_{1-27} are the Level 2 coefficients for the listed independent variables (any variable with a ".j" ending is the classroom average of students for that variable); and

* u is a Level 2 random effect.

The multilevel models described in Chapter Six are simple "fixed co-efficient" models (Kreft and DeLeeuw, 1998). The coefficients for the Level 1 relationships between student characteristics and achievement scores are held constant across classrooms. There are no cross-level interactions between classroom and student characteristics. Thus, between-classroom differences are limited to differences in intercepts. In other words, the intercept for each classroom is the sum of the overall intercept and the sums of the classroom aggregate variables weighted by the classroom-level regression coefficients, plus random error. The achievement score of each student then is the sum of that student's classroom intercept and the sum of the student-level coefficients, plus error (Koretz, McCaffrey, and Sullivan, 2001).

Student-level variables were centered on their classroom-level means. Centering is particularly important for these Level 1 variables both for interpretation of the intercept as well as to ensure numerical stability (Bryk and Raudenbush, 1992, p. 25). Without centering, one would interpret the intercept as the expected outcome for a student in classroom j who has a value of zero on all the Level 1 predictor variables, which often does not have meaning. With centering, one can interpret the intercept as the expected outcome for a student in classroom j who is at the mean of all the predictor variables. Dummy variables were also group-mean centered; thus the intercept term is the adjusted mean outcome in classroom j, adjusted for differences among units in the percentages of students with various characteristics. The group (classroom) means of the student-level variables were then included in the Level 2 model to avoid the assumption that the effects of variations in classroom means equal the effects of deviations within classrooms (Bryk and Raudenbush, 1992). This specification also makes the overall model's coefficients straightforward estimates of the within- and between-classroom effects.[1]

---

[1]Cohen et al. (1998) point out the importance of reintroducing the classroom means when the Level 1 variables are group-mean centered. They argue that a model in which the (Level 1) variables are centered on their classroom means sheds an important piece of information: the classroom mean of the variable. Specifically, they write, "When the analyst fails to re-introduce this source of systematic variation appropriately elsewhere in the model, he or she posits that the actual value of the centered does not influence the outcome, only the relative value (that is, relative to the school [or classroom in this context] mean)" (pp. 18–19).

MULTILEVEL RESULTS FOR THE RELATIONSHIPS OF 1998 TEST SCORES TO STUDENT, CLASSROOM, AND SCHOOL FACTORS IN FOURTH GRADE SAMPLE

Table B.1

Multilevel Results for the Relationships of 1998 Test Scores to Student, Classroom, and School Factors in Fourth Grade Sample

| | Stanford-9 Reading | | | | TAAS Reading | | | | TAAS Mathematics | | | |
| | Model 1 | | Model 2 | | Model 1 | | Model 2 | | Model 1 | | Model 2 | |
Variables	Coef.	SE	Coef.	SE	Coef.	SE	Coef.	SE	Coef.	SE	Coef.	SE
	Independent Variables for Students (n = 861)											
Intercept	1.77	5.02	1.30	4.86	1.05	4.15	-1.75	4.00	9.02	4.61	4.71	4.28
Male	-0.29[a]	0.06	-0.28[a]	0.06	0.01	0.05	0.01	0.05	-0.01	0.05	-0.01	0.05
African American	-0.09	0.11	-0.10	0.11	-0.13	0.09	-0.14	0.09	-0.15	0.09	-0.15	0.09
White or other	0.17	0.11	0.18	0.11	0.11	0.09	0.11	0.09	-0.02	0.09	-0.02	0.09
Bilingual education program	0.48[b]	0.23	0.48[b]	0.23	0.04	0.19	0.04	0.19	-0.25	0.18	-0.25	0.18
Limited English proficiency	0.14	0.12	0.14	0.12	-0.03	0.10	-0.03	0.10	-0.21[b]	0.10	-0.21[b]	0.10
Free/reduced price lunch program eligible	-0.03	0.11	-0.03	0.11	-0.02	0.10	-0.02	0.10	0.14	0.09	0.14	0.09
Special education	-0.37[a]	0.10	-0.37[a]	0.10	-0.52[a]	0.09	-0.52[a]	0.09	-0.52[a]	0.08	-0.52[a]	0.08
Gifted and talented education	0.34[a]	0.12	0.34[a]	0.12	0.60[a]	0.10	0.60[a]	0.10	0.47[a]	0.09	0.47[a]	0.09
Age	-0.15[b]	0.07	-0.15[b]	0.07	-0.08	0.06	-0.08	0.06	-0.10	0.05	-0.10	0.05
Weeks in classroom	0.01	0.00	0.01	0.00	0.01[b]	0.00	0.01[b]	0.00	0.00	0.00	0.00	0.00
1997 TAAS reading score	0.31[a]	0.04	0.31[a]	0.04	0.53[a]	0.03	0.53[a]	0.03	—[c]	—[c]	—[c]	—[c]
1997 TAAS mathematics score	—[c]	—[c]	—[c]	—[c]	—[c]	—[c]	—[c]	—[c]	0.59[a]	0.03	0.59[a]	0.03
Missing 1997 TAAS reading score	-0.06	0.10	-0.07	0.10	-0.02	0.09	-0.02	0.09	—[c]	—[c]	—[c]	—[c]
Missing 1997 TAAS mathematics score	—[c]	—[c]	—[c]	—[c]	—[c]	—[c]	—[c]	—[c]	-0.08	0.08	-0.08	0.08
	Independent Variables for Classrooms (n = 63)											
Male	-0.68	0.42	-0.74	0.43	-0.53	0.35	-0.59	0.35	-0.07	0.35	-0.36	0.33
African American	-0.10	0.28	0.34	0.31	-0.23	0.23	0.07	0.25	-0.26	0.24	-0.01	0.24
White or other	-0.49	0.48	-0.46	0.47	0.34	0.39	0.42	0.38	-0.19	0.43	-0.04	0.39
Bilingual education program	-0.22	0.25	-0.21	0.24	-0.29	0.21	-0.38	0.20	-0.05	0.20	-0.20	0.19
Limited English proficiency	-0.26	0.50	-0.28	0.51	-0.06	0.41	-0.08	0.42	-0.42	0.42	-0.37	0.39
Free/reduced price lunch program eligible	-0.07	0.54	-0.21	0.54	-0.57	0.44	-0.41	0.44	-0.40	0.45	0.08	0.42
Special education	0.36	0.55	0.36	0.55	-0.73	0.45	-0.84	0.45	-0.57	0.47	-0.67	0.42
Gifted and talented education	0.99[b]	0.49	1.17[b]	0.46	0.20	0.40	0.21	0.38	0.54	0.42	0.61	0.37
Age	-0.30	0.41	-0.40	0.41	-0.18	0.34	-0.06	0.33	-0.84[b]	0.37	-0.59	0.35
Weeks in classroom	0.04	0.03	0.04	0.03	0.02	0.02	0.03	0.02	-0.02	0.03	-0.01	0.02

Table B.1 (continued)

Variables	Stanford-9 Reading				TAAS Reading				TAAS Mathematics			
	Model 1		Model 2		Model 1		Model 2		Model 1		Model 2	
	Coef.	SE	Coef.	SE	Coef.	SE	Coef.	SE	Coef.	SE	Coef.	SE
1997 TAAS reading score	0.33	0.16	0.32	0.16	0.46[a]	0.14	0.40[a]	0.13	—[c]	—[c]	—[c]	—[c]
1997 TAAS Mathematics Score	—[c]	—[c]	—[c]	—[c]	—[c]	—[c]	—[c]	—[c]	0.71[a]	0.14	0.60[a]	0.13
Missing 1997 TAAS reading score	0.40	0.44	0.06	0.44	-0.46	0.36	-0.54	0.36	—[c]	—[c]	—[c]	—[c]
Missing 1997 TAAS mathematics score	—[c]	—[c]	—[c]	—[c]	—[c]	—[c]	—[c]	—[c]	-0.59	0.39	-0.56	0.36
Male teacher	0.37	0.20	0.34	0.20	0.02	0.17	-0.09	0.16	-0.31	0.18	-0.34[b]	0.16
African American teacher	-0.02	0.14	-0.17	0.14	0.04	0.12	-0.01	0.11	-0.06	0.12	-0.11	0.11
White or other teacher	-0.10	0.11	-0.09	0.11	-0.05	0.09	0.04	0.09	-0.20[b]	0.10	-0.13	0.09
Years of teaching experience	0.02[a]	0.01	0.02[a]	0.01	0.01[a]	0.01	0.02[a]	0.00	0.00	0.01	0.01	0.00
Master's degree	-0.22[b]	0.10	-0.18	0.09	-0.22[a]	0.08	-0.21[b]	0.08	-0.03	0.08	-0.03	0.07
Instructional strategies:												
Lecture	—[c]	—[c]	-0.03	0.05	—[c]	—[c]	0.03	0.04	—[c]	—[c]	0.00	0.04
Students work individually on written assignments / worksheets in class	—[c]	—[c]	0.08	0.09	—[c]	—[c]	0.07	0.08	—[c]	—[c]	0.15[b]	0.07
Students practice or drill on computational skills	—[c]	—[c]	0.14	0.08	—[c]	—[c]	0.07	0.06	—[c]	—[c]	0.12	0.06
Teacher survey indices:												
Collegiality	—[c]	—[c]	-0.03	0.07	—[c]	—[c]	-0.08	0.06	—[c]	—[c]	-0.15	0.06
Principal leadership	—[c]	—[c]	0.12	0.09	—[c]	—[c]	0.15[b]	0.07	—[c]	—[c]	0.21	0.07
Quality of professional development	—[c]	—[c]	0.17	0.09	—[c]	—[c]	0.05	0.07	—[c]	—[c]	-0.02	0.07
Reform	—[c]	—[c]	0.11	0.11	—[c]	—[c]	0.03	0.09	—[c]	—[c]	0.13	0.09
Teacher's perceptions of factors hindering student achievement	—[c]	—[c]	-0.02	0.08	—[c]	—[c]	0.11	0.06	—[c]	—[c]	0.09	0.06
Independent Variables for Schools (n = 23)												
Average Texas Education Agency rank, 1995–1997	0.06	0.25	0.02	0.25	0.50[b]	0.20	0.30	0.21	0.44[b]	0.22	0.12	0.20
Years implementing a NAS design	-0.06	0.08	-0.04	0.08	-0.06	0.07	-0.05	0.07	-0.14	0.07	-0.13	0.07

NOTE: SE is standard error.

[a] Significant at 0.01 level.

[b] Significant at 0.05 level.

[c] Excluded from the model.

BIBLIOGRAPHY

Berends, M. (1999). *Assessing New American Schools: A status report.* Santa Monica, CA: RAND.

Berends, M. (2000). Teacher-reported effects of New American Schools designs: Exploring the relationships to teacher background and school context. *Educational Evaluation and Policy Analysis,* 22(1), 65–82.

Berends, M., Grissmer, D. W., Kirby, S. N., & Williamson, S. (1999). The changing American family and student achievement trends. *Review of Sociology of Education and Socialization,* 23, 67–101.

Berends, M., & King, M. B. (1994). A description of restructuring in nationally nominated schools: The legacy of the iron cage? *Educational Policy,* 8(1), 28–50. (Also RAND RP-458).

Berends, M., Kirby, S. N., Naftel, S., & McKelvey, C. (2001). *Implementation and performance in New American Schools: Three years into scale-up.* Santa Monica, CA: RAND.

Bodilly, S. (2001). *New American Schools' concept of break the mold designs: How designs evolved and why.* Santa Monica, CA: RAND.

Bodilly, S. J. (1998). *Lessons from New American Schools' scale-up phase: Prospects for bringing designs to multiple schools.* Santa Monica, CA: RAND (MR-1777-NAS).

Bodilly, S. J., & Berends, M. (1999). Necessary district support for comprehensive school reform. In G. Orfield & E. H. DeBray (Eds.), *Hard work for good schools: Facts not fads in Title I reform* (pp.

111–119). Boston , MA: The Civil Rights Project, Harvard University.

Bohrnstedt, G. W., & Stecher, B. M. (Eds.). (1999). *Class size reduction in California: Early evaluation findings, 1996–1998.* Sacramento, CA: California Department of Education.

Borman, K. M., Cookson, P. W., Jr., Sadovnik, A. R., and Spade, J. Z. (Eds.). (1996). *Implementing educational reform: Sociological perspectives on educational policy.* Norwood, NJ.: Ablex Publishing Corporation.

Brookover, W. B., Beady, C., Flood, P., Schewitzer, J., & Wisenbaker, J. (1979). *School social systems and student achievement: Schools can make a difference.* New York: Praeger.

Bryk, A. S., Lee, V., & Holland, P. (1993). *Catholic schools and the common good.* Cambridge, MA: Harvard University.

Bryk, A. S., & Raudenbush, S. (1992). *Hierarchical linear models: Applications and data analysis methods.* Newbury Park, CA: Sage Publications.

Bryk, A. S., Raudenbush, S. W., & Congdon, R. T. (1996). *HLM: Hierarchical linear and nonlinear modeling with the HLM/2L and HLM/3L programs.* Chicago: Scientific Software International.

Burstein, L., McDonnell, L. M., Van Winkle, J., Ormseth, T., Mirocha, J., & Guitton, G. (1995). *Validating national curriculum indicators.* Santa Monica, CA: RAND.

Clune, W. (1998). *Toward a theory of systemic reform: The case of nine NSF statewide systemic initiatives.* Madison, WI: Wisconsin Center for Education Research, University of Wisconsin-Madison.

Cohen, D., & Hill, H. C. (2000). Instructional policy and classroom performance: The mathematics reform in California. *Teachers College Record*, 102(2), 294–343.

Cohen, J., Baldi, S., & Rathbun, A. (1998). Hierarchical linear models and their application in educational research. Unpublished manuscript, American Institutes for Research, Washington, DC.

Coleman, J. S., Campbell, E. Q., Hobson, C. J., McPartland, J., Mood, A. M., Weinfeld, F. D., & York, R. L. (1966). *Equality of educational opportunity.* Washington, DC: U.S. Government Printing Office.

Consortium for Policy Research in Education. (1998). *States and districts and comprehensive school reform.* CPRE Policy Brief. Philadelphia, PA: University of Pennsylvania Graduate School of Education.

Datnow, A. (1998). *The gender politics of educational change.* London: Falmer Press.

Datnow, A. (2000a). Gender politics and school reform. In A. Hargreaves & N. Bascia (Eds.), *The sharp edge of change: Teaching, leading, and the realities of reform.* London: Falmer Press.

Datnow, A. (2000b). Power and politics in the adoption of school reform models. *Educational Evaluation and Policy Analysis, 22*(4), 357–374.

Datnow, A., & Castellano, J. (2000). Teachers' responses to Success for All: How beliefs, experiences, and adaptations shape implementation. *American Educational Research Journal, 37*(3), 775–799.

Datnow, A., & Stringfield, S. (2000). Working together for reliable school reform. *Journal of Education for Students Placed At Risk, 5*(1), 183–204.

Desimone, L. (2000). *Making comprehensive school reform work.* New York: ERIC Clearinghouse on Urban Education.

Edmonds, R. R. (1979). Effective schools for the urban poor. *Educational Leadership, 37,* 15–27.

Fordham, S., & Ogbu, J. (1986). Black students' school success: Coping with the burden of acting white. *Urban Review, 18*(3), 176–206.

Foster, M. (1993). Resisting racism: Personal testimonies of African-American teachers. In L. Weis & M. Fine (Eds.), *Beyond silenced voices: Class, race, and gender in United States schools* (pp. 273–288). Albany, NY: State University of New York Press.

Fullan, M. G. (2001). *The new meaning of educational change,* third edition. New York: Teachers College Press.

Gamoran, A. (1987). The stratification of high school learning opportunities. *Sociology of Education,* 60, 135–155.

Gamoran, A. (1992). The variable effects of high school tracking. *American Sociological Review,* 57, 812–828.

Gamoran, A., Nystrand, M., Berends, M., & LePore, P. C. (1995). An organizational analysis of the effects of ability grouping. *American Educational Research Journal,* 32, 687–715.

Gamoran, A., Porter, A. C., Smithson, J., & White, P. A. (1997). Upgrading high school mathematics instruction: Improving learning opportunities for low-achieving, low-income youth. *Educational Evaluation and Policy Analysis,* 19(4), 325–338.

Garet, J. S., Birman, B. F., Porter, A. C., Desimone, L., Herman, R., & Yoon, K. S. (1999). *Designing effective professional development: Lessons from the Eisenhower program.* Washington, DC: U.S. Department of Education.

Glennan, T. K., Jr. (1998). *New American Schools after six years.* Santa Monica, CA: RAND (MR-945-NASDC).

Greene, W. H. (2000). *Economic analysis,* fourth edition. Upper Saddle River, NJ: Prentice Hall.

Grissmer, D. (Ed.). (1999). Special issue on class size, issues and new findings. *Educational Evaluation and Policy Analysis,* 21(2).

Herman, R., Aladjem, D., McMahon, P., Masem, E., Mulligan, I., Smith O'Malley, A., Quinones, S., Reeve, A., & Woodruff, D. (1999). *An educators' guide to schoolwide reform.* Washington, DC: American Institutes for Research.

Hoffer, T. (1992). Effects of community type on school experiences and student learning. Paper presented to the 1992 annual meeting of the American Educational Research Association, San Francisco.

Huberman, M. (1989). The professional life cycle of teachers. *Teachers College Record,* 91(2), 30–57.

Jencks, C. S., Smith, M., Acland, H., Bane, M. J., Cohen, D., Gintis, H., Heyns, B., & Michelson, S. (1972). *Inequality: A reassessment of the effect of family and schooling in America.* New York: Basic Books.

Keltner, B. (1998). *Resources for transforming New American Schools: First year findings.* Santa Monica, CA: RAND (IP-175).

Kirby, S. N., Berends, M., & Naftel, S. (2001). *Implementation in a longitudinal sample of New American Schools: Four years into scale-up.* Santa Monica, CA: RAND (MR-1413-EDU).

Kirby, S. N., Sloan-McCombs, J. S., Naftel, S., & Berends, M. (In Review). *Title I schools receiving Comprehensive School Reform Demonstration (CSRD) funds: Recent evidence from the National Longitudinal Survey of Schools.* Washington, DC: U.S. Department of Education.

Klein, S., Hamilton, L., McCaffrey, D., Stecher, B., Robyn, A., & Burroughs, D. (2000). *Teaching practices and student achievement: Report of first-year findings from the "Mosaic Study" of Systemic Initiatives in Mathematics and Science.* Santa Monica, CA: RAND (MR-1233-EDU).

Koretz, D. M. (1996). Using student assessments for educational accountability. In E. A. Hanushek & D. W. Jorgenson (Eds.), *Improving America's schools: The role of incentives* (pp. 171–196). Washington, DC: National Academy Press.

Koretz, D. M., & Barron, S. I. (1998). *The validity of gains in scores on the Kentucky Instructional Results Information System (KIRIS).* Santa Monica, CA: RAND (MR-1014-EDU).

Koretz, D. M., McCaffrey, D., & Sullivan, T. (2001). *Using TIMSS to analyze correlates of performance variation in mathematics.* NCES Working Paper 2001-05. Washington, DC: National Center for Education Statistics, U.S. Department of Education.

Kreft, I., & De Leeuw, J. (1998). *Introducing multilevel modeling.* London: Sage Publications.

Lee, V. E., & Bryk, A. S. (1989). A multilevel model of the social distribution of high school achievement. *Sociology of Education*, 51, 78–94.

Lee, V. E., Loeb, S., & Lubeck, S. (1998). Contextual effects of prekindergarten classroom for disadvantaged children on cognitive development: The case of Chapter 1. *Child Development*, 69(2), 479–494.

Lippman, L., Burns, S., & McArthur, E. (1996). *Urban schools: The challenge of location and poverty.* Washington, DC: National Center for Education Statistics, U.S. Department of Education.

Louis, K. S., Kruse, S. D., & Marks, H. M. (1996). Schoolwide professional community. In F. M. Newmann (Ed.), *Authentic achievement: Restructuring schools for intellectual quality* (pp. 179–203). San Francisco: Jossey-Bass Publishers.

Louis, K. S., & Marks, H. M. (1998). Does professional community affect the classroom? Teachers' work and student experiences in restructuring schools. *American Journal of Education*, 106(4), 532–575.

Marks, H. M., Newmann, F. M., & Gamoran, A. (1996). Does authentic pedagogy increase student achievement? In F. M. Newmann (Ed.), *Authentic achievement: Restructuring schools for intellectual quality* (pp. 49–73). San Francisco: Jossey-Bass Publishers.

Mayer, D. P. (1999). Measuring instructional practice: Can policymakers trust survey data? *Educational Evaluation and Policy Analysis*, 21(1), 29–45.

McLaughlin, M. W. (1990). The RAND Change Agent study revisited: Macro perspectives and micro realities. *Educational Researcher*, 19(9), 11–16.

Meyer, R. H. (1996). Value-added indicators of school performance. In E. A. Hanushek & D. W. Jorgenson (Eds.), *Improving America's schools: The role of incentives* (pp. 197–224). Washington, DC: National Academy Press.

Montjoy, R., & O'Toole, L. (1979). Toward a theory of policy implementation: An organizational perspective. *Public Administration Review*, 465–476.

New American Schools Development Corporation. (1997). *Bringing success to scale: Sharing the vision of New American Schools.* Arlington, VA: Author.

New American Schools Development Corporation. (1991). *Designs for a new generation of American schools: Request for proposals.* Arlington, VA: Author.

Newmann, F. M., & Associates. (Ed.) (1996). *Authentic achievement: Restructuring schools for intellectual quality.* San Francisco: Jossey-Bass Publishers.

Oakes, J., Gamoran, A., & Page, R. N. (1992). Curriculum differentiation: Opportunities, outcomes, and meanings. In P. W. Jackson (Ed.), *Handbook of research on curriculum* (pp. 570–608). New York: Macmillan.

Porter, A. C. (1994). National standards and school improvement in the 1990s: Issues and promise. *American Journal of Education*, 102(4), 421–449.

Porter, A. C. (1995). *Developing opportunity-to-learn indicators of the content of instruction.* Madison, WI: Wisconsin Center for Education Research, University of Wisconsin-Madison.

Porter, A. C., Floden, R., Freeman, D., Schmidt, W., & Schwille, J. (1988). Content determinants in elementary school mathematics. In D. A. Grouws & T. J. Cooney (Eds.), *Perspectives on research on effective mathematics teaching* (pp. 96–113). Hillsdale, NJ: Erlbaum.

Porter, A. C., Kirst, M. W., Osthoff, E. J., Smithson, J. L., Schneider, S. A. (1993). *Reform up close: An analysis of high school mathematics and science classrooms.* Madison, WI: Wisconsin Center for Education Research, University of Wisconsin-Madison.

Porter, A. C., & Smithson, J. L. (1995). *Enacted curriculum survey items catalogue: Middle school and high school mathematics and science.* Madison, WI: Wisconsin Center for Education Research, University of Wisconsin-Madison.

Puma, J. M., Karweit, N., Price, C., Ricciuti, A., Vaden-Kiernan, M. (1997). *Prospects: Final report on student outcomes.* Bethesda, MD: Abt Associates.

Purkey, S. C., & Smith, M. S. (1983). Effective schools: A review. *Elementary School Journal,* 83(4), 427–452.

Ralph, J. (1990). A research agenda on effective school for disadvantaged students. In S. S. Goldberg (Ed.), *Readings on equal education, volume 10: Critical issues for a new administration and congress.* New York: AMS Press.

Ross, S., Troutman, A., Horgan, D., Maxwell, S., Laitinen, R., & Lowther, D. (1997). The success of schools in implementing eight restructuring designs: A synthesis of first year evaluation outcomes. *School Effectiveness and School Improvement,* 8(1), 95–124.

Ross, S. M., Sanders, W. L., Wright, S. P., Stringfield, S., Wang, W., & Alberg, M. (2001). Two- and three-year achievement results from the Memphis restructuring initiative. *School Effectiveness and School Improvement,* 12(3), 265–284.

Singer, J. D. (1998). Using SAS PROC MIXED to fit multilevel models, hierarchical models, and individual growth models. *Journal of Educational and Behavioral Statistics,* 24(4), 323–355.

Smith, L., Ross, S., McNelis, M., Squires, M., Wasson, R., Maxwell, S., Weddle, W., Nath, L., Grehan, A., & Buggey, T. (1998). The Memphis Restructuring Initiative: Analysis of activities and outcomes that impact implementation success. *Education and Urban Society,* 30(3), 296–325.

Smith, M. S., Scoll, B. W., & Link, J. (1996). Research-based school reform: The Clinton administration's agenda. In E. A. Hanushek & D. W. Jorgenson (Eds.), *Improving America's schools: The role of incentives* (pp. 9–27). Washington, DC: National Academy Press.

Stecher, B. M., & Bohrnstedt, G. W. (Eds). (2000). *Class size reduction in California: The 1998–99 evaluation findings.* Sacramento, CA: California Department of Education.

Stringfield, S. (1998). Choosing success. *American Educator,* 46, 13–17.

Texas Education Agency. (1999). School size and class size in Texas public schools. *Policy Research Report,* No. 13.

U.S. Department of Education. (1993). *Improving America's Schools Act of 1993: The reauthorization of the Elementary and Secondary Education Act and other amendments.* Washington, DC: Author.

Weatherly, R., & Lipsky, M. (1977). Street-level bureaucrats and institutional innovation: Implementing special education reform. *Harvard Education Review,* 47(2), 171–197.

Wong, K., & Meyer, S. (1998). Title I school-wide programs: A synthesis of findings from recent evaluation. *Educational Evaluation and Policy Analysis,* 20(2), 115–136.

Yonezawa, S., & Datnow, A. (1999). Supporting multiple reform designs in a culturally and linguistically diverse school district. *Journal of Education for Students Placed at Risk,* 4(1), 101–125.